Colombian Blood

Andolian Napraja

ISBN: 1517239354
ISBN-13: 978-1517239350

DEDICATION

I dedicate this book to all the former members of El Santa Muerte and Junior Cartel--all my "brothers and "sisters" who were a part of that legacy. B.I.L.-B.I.D.!

This is also dedicated to my beloved aunt Griselda Blanco. May you rest in peace and watch over me.

ACKNOWLEDGMENTS

My father, Juan Andolian Ochoa-Napraja of Medellin, Columbia, and my mother, Rosalyn Martin, also known as "Columbian Roz." To my most loyal brother and 1st Apostle, Tozerria "Ocean" McClendon who always stood by me no matter what. Por Siempre! The Infamous Paper Boy still lives...

Second, I want to thank my friend, Michael Larsen, co-founder of the Larsen Pomeda Literary Agency in San Francisco. If it wasn't for you, none of this would be possible. Thank you for all the help over the years while I was in prison and everything you've done for me since I've been home. You have been more than a friend to me. Thank you for believing in me!

Third, my friend and publishing guide over at CriminalU.co, A. Scot Bolsinger, for believing in me and my work since day one. Thank you for all the support you raised for this book and thr strategic insight behind it's development. To those editors, artists, and support people who I haven't even yet met, I thank you all!

Fourth, my beautiful girlfriend LaTasha White, for all your love and support. My younger brothers Paris Martin and Quashaun Thomas. My two cousins, Antonio "Boo Gotti" Burrell and Chris "L.C." Lawrence for your love and devoted loyalty. Can't forget my cousin Kente, "Man" Burrell and his wife Erica Evans. Nothing but love for both of you. And my brother from another mother, Jovanni "Muhammad" Vernon-Bey. Much love.

This also goes out to all my homies locked up in federal and state prison (MDOC). Shout out to Ricardo Richard, one of the realest brothers I ever met. My big brother, Dennis "Blackaveli" Farmer-El. My cousin, Errol Martin on lock down Hold your head. I got you! Shout out to all my latinos across the world. My story, "Junior Cartel: The rise of the Infamous Paper Boy," is coming soon.

And last, my brother and partner, Dominic "Shawn" Redman, a.k.a. Lennox and his girlfriend and my sister Tera Brown, my boy Ladon "Meech" Clark and my other homie J.G. on lockdown in Anderson, Indiana. Shout out to my boy Indiana Juice and my girl Valencia "Vivi" Stennis. All my homies in the small town of Anderson, Indiana. My boy Roger Randolph, bother of NBA star Zack Randolph of the Memphis Grizzlies. Much love, bro! It's your boy, Babyface Juan.

Andolian Napraja

Prologue
Detroit-1998

The growling Motor City wind whistled in through the cracks of her car window as her black 7-Series came to a halt at the corner of the residential street. She could see the home from where she sat, a middle-class custom-built brick house. It was dark on the street. Deserted, so it seemed.

In the car, she readied herself, searching the rearview mirror, studying her reflection. Her almost black eyes stared back at her long bloody-red hair and analyzed her face. Confident everything was intact, she exited the car.

Brutal cold greeted her, about 10-below zero with a jaw-wrenching wind chill. Snow illuminated the surface around her and made crunching sounds with every step she made in her sleek black suede and gold-buckled Dior boots.

She dressed meticulously even on a night like this. Every article of clothing had to be perfectly coordinated with her personality, occupation and lifestyle.

On this night, she decided on an all-white, double-breasted belted cashmere coat over a nearly floor-length black Christian Dior dress. A matching black alligator handbag finished it off. Any fashion expert would have been impressed.

She strolled up the street, unfazed by the icy temperature. When she reached the front door, she rang the doorbell and waited.

* * * * *

Those dreaded "middle years" pursued Eva Azaria, who suffered from the stress of nearly every woman not aging as gracefully as desired.

The image in the mirror did nothing to diminish her insecurities. Her hair looked like something out of a horror movie, strands in every direction. Lines had begun to crevice under her dark eyes. Even at five-seven and still thin, she never showed off her legs like she once had. Eva felt like a cigarette burning at both ends, like her world was slowly coming to an end and she was unable to stall it.

Her husband showed less interest in her day by day. She loved Jose, but she wasn't a fool. He didn't even look at her the same. Over the last few months, she surprised herself at seriously considering plastic surgery, but feared her two children would hate her for it when they were older. It wasn't something a woman should do to try to preserve her youth, Eva knew this, or at least told herself she did.

She groped in her large walk-in closet for something to throw on when she heard the sound of the doorbell, ringing like a wall clock. She grabbed the first thing that looked warm and comfortable, threw it on, then made her way out to the living room where Jose had been sitting watching *Sabado Gigante* on television.

The lamp light and the television dimly lit the room as she entered. The emptiness of the room startled her. Eva opened the front door, searching for Jose out on the front porch, but was met only by the freezing wind. Confused, she stepped back into the house and pushed the door shut.

"Jose?" she called out.

Nothing, except the faint sound of rapid Spanish coming from the television. She flicked the TV off and listened.

She heard nothing.

"Jose?" she called out again.

Nothing. Then a small vibration of her pulse rising.

She cautiously entered the dining room, only to find it empty as well. Turning the corner to the kitchen the anxious noise of the known and the unknown shattered the quiet. Her eyes fell on her Jose lying on his stomach in the middle of the kitchen floor. Eva rushed to his side and yanked him over on his back. Glazed eyes stared back. A bullet hole rested in the center of his forehead.

Her scream joined the howl of the wind outside.

"Ohh, noo, Jose! Who did this to you? Why did they do this?" she wept, her tears dotting her husband's grey shirt until her watery eyes caught a ghost-like image, wearing a double-breasted, belted cashmere coat.

"Who are you? Why? Why did you take my Jose away from me?" Eva yelled.

The woman stood before here without emotion.

"Who are you, you bitch?" Eva shouted.

The female assassin answered with a raised chrome 9mm auto, equipped with a sound suppressor.

With her last breath, Eva thanked God that her son and daughter had been away for the weekend at her sister's house. She prayed they would be okay. She prayed their killer wouldn't harm their dear children. She prayed, the assassin fired.

PHFT! PHFT!

And it was silent.

Andolian Napraja

Chapter One

With a shrill, the small radio alarm clock resting on the nightstand exploded, ringing loudly in Ghost's ears, waking him up. He rolled over in bed and hit the snooze button. After a pause, he stretched his arms in the air, yawning.

The strong aroma of his mother frying bacon and eggs downstairs finished the alarm clock's job, fully awakening him and his hunger.

After a quick shower, Ghost dressed in the bedroom, throwing on a pair of sanded bronze and red LRG denim jeans, a black and red striped, long-sleeve, wrinkle-resistant shirt, an Mauri alligator-top and leather-sided shoes. His attire wasn't complete without its main accessory. He reached under his pillow, removed a nickel-plated .45 and stuck it in his waistband, then followed the home-cooked smell of breakfast downstairs.

Emilia, his mother, stood over the stove with a spoon in her hand, stirring a pot filled with grits. She was a small woman with long, silky black hair pulled neatly into a tight ponytail with a blue bow on the end. A perfect image of an ideal Colombian woman, straight out of the hills of the old country.

His mother must have felt his presence behind her. Without turning around to face him, she sternly said, "buenos dios, Ricardo. Tu Hambre?"

Ghost just smiled and wondered to himself how did his mother do that? He shook his head in disbelief. "Si, madre. Gracias. Huele bien!"

"Sentar," she instructed.

Ghost sat down at the granite countertop island in the kitchen while his mother began making him a plate of breakfast.

Emilia held up a bottle of Sunny Delight. "Zumo?"

He nodded and made an approval sort of hum, and she poured him some juice.

"So ..." she said in broken English. "You're going out to find a job today, yes?"

He looked at his mother and burst into a roar of laughter "Yeah right, ma. You know me better than that! I got better things to do, then to be working at somebody's low-wage paying company."

His mother giggled at his honesty. She knew damn well he wasn't about to go get any job. That wasn't what their family was into. It was just something to say that they both could start their day off laughing at.

"Just kidding, hijo," Emilia said grinning at him. Oh, how much he reminded her of her husband. Same attitude. Same rounded dark-hued face, sharp no-nonsense eyes and broad shoulders on a strong physique.

The only significant difference between the two was that Ghost kept his hair cut low-tapered on the sides, while his father's hair was typically longer and combed backwards with thick Caribbean curls at the top. "Well, what is it that you plan on doing with your day?" She asked, this time serious.

"I got a few rounds to make," he said as he took a swig of the orange juice. "See if I can link up with this crew out in southwest Detroit that's gettin' money."

His mother knew exactly what he meant by linking up, but she wondered what crew he was referring to. "Which one?"

Ghost smirked as he got up and kissed his mother goodbye. "I'll tell you later," he said over his shoulder, heading out the front door.

It was a nice summer day outside. The temperature couldn't have been more perfect. Ghost eased his way over to his 1969 cherry and black rally-striped Chevy Camaro on black-and-red 26-inch Asanti rims. The car sat high in the air like a spider on four thick legs. He loved the attention it brought when he went to the hood. It made him feel like he was starring in a rap video.

He got in and fired the engine up, listening to the machine's big-block roar, feeling the vibration of the beast that only he was in control of.

Not wanting to wait any longer, Ghost gently pulled out his parents' round driveway, then swerved away like a bat out of hell, the tires screeching. "Urrr!"

It was eleven-thirty when he arrived on the east side of Detroit, and the streets were already beginning to come alive with traffic and people walking in all directions, starting their morning off.

Ghost effortlessly pushed the purring Camaro up the busy intersection, listening to "Controversy," a track by Scrill, one of Detroit's hottest rappers. His volume was cranked up to the maximum, rattling the trunk, the bass pounding like the heartbeat of a giant.

He made a left turn down a residential street and slowed his pace as his eyes searched the houses, looking for the address he had written on a piece of paper.

There was a small crowd up the block, hanging in a driveway. Ghost wondered was that the location he was looking for.

A few stares came from some of the girls and guys standing out front as he stopped the car across the street from all the action.

He matched the address with the numbers on the paper, took a deep breath, then parked the Camaro.

The house was made of gray painted brick and white aluminum siding.

Apparently there was an early morning dice game transpiring. Five guys and four girls were in a circle near the side of the house. Ghost got out the car and leaned against the passenger door, observing the action.

"SEVEN!" A short, dark nigga in a white T-shirt and blue jeans shouted. "Pass the dice."

Ghost crossed his arms and watched intently when he recognized a familiar face appear in the crowd, casually dressed in a navy short sleeve Gucci shirt, and black V-noch-waist plain front pants, a leather band and diamond bezel watch neatly rested on his wrist.

It was the man he had come to see. The notorious Juan Azaria, one of Detroit's most infamous drug dealers. He and his sister, Ayana, had been holding it down for the last few years and were really coming up in the world.

Ghost needed to speak to him.

Juan had a smooth, laid-back persona, he was medium-height, averagely built, with wavy jet black hair. He nodded his head at Ghost when he peeped him leaning against the Camaro's door.

Ghost returned a nod and folded his arms, continuing to wait patiently as Juan grabbed the dice from the last shooter.

He tossed the dice and they bounced off the brick of the house and hit the concrete pavement, spinning.

Everybody's eyes were glued on the little ivory cubes, not a word was uttered.

"FOUR!" said the same short nigga, shaking his head.

"All right," Juan held up a hand filled with money. "Who's gonna fade me?"

"I got you. Bet a thousand." A dark-brown skinned brother with a bald head spoke up.

Ghost had seen him a couple times before around Juan. His name was Rasco; an up-and-coming heroin dealer who ran one of the east side crews. He ruled his area with an iron fist and was respected by half the city. "What, that's too much for you, nigga?"

Juan giggled at that. "Muthafucka, please! That ain't shit! Put two thousand out there."

He shook the dice and then threw them with skill.

Once again they slapped against the brick wall and hit the ground rolling, but this time, the dice stopped quickly.

"ALL, HELL NO!" the short guy cried out.

"FOUR!" someone shouted.

"Give me my damn money!" Juan started picking up the pile of bills and stuffing his pockets. "Got me out here early in the morning fuckin' with y'all fools."

Ghost began walking over toward the crowd that was now dispersing.

Juan gave Ghost a greeting five and an embrace. "So what you wanna holla at me about?"

He hesitated for a minute, contemplating his thoughts before he spoke. He knew Juan was a shrewd businessman and could easily distinguish weakness from strength, so he had to be on point. "I told you the last time we spoke that I been doing a little trappin' out in Traverse City, right?"

Juan nodded his head, but said nothing.

"Well, shit is really starting to pick up. I got a small crew and everything now."

"So what's the problem?" Juan asked, trying to figure out where he fit in.

Ghost inhaled deeply. "Let me finish."

Juan waved his hand and sighed. "My fault, homie. Please continue."

"Like I was saying … I got a crew now, and we making a lot of noise up there, and a lot of money too, but I need to get my hands on some of that good coke you got, and I can sew the whole city up."

"How much work you talking about?"

"At least two bricks."

Juan adjusted his posture, putting his right hand under his chin, his fingers massaging the hairs on his perfectly lined beard. "What's the turnover time? How long would it take you to get rid of that much product?"

"A week at best." Ghost shot at him quickly.

"How much money you workin' with?"

"All I got is thirty-five thousand right now."

"That ain't enough for two keys. Not in today's market," Juan told him sternly. "You need at least sixty stacks."

Ghost shook his head. "Look, I know that. But I was thinking, maybe you want a piece of the action, too. So I figured we can be partners. All you have to do is give me the work, I'll handle all the business, and we'll split everything fifty-fifty."

He could tell Juan was feeling the idea, he just stood there with a stupid grin across his lips, rubbing his chin. "All right," he finally said. "Meet me back here in an hour, and I'll give you what you're asking for. But dawg, this shit is serious. You can't fuck up."

Ghost looked him dead in the eye, and said, "I got this bro. Trust me."

While he was waiting, he decided to cruise around the city so that he could think and plan his next move. Now that he was about to link up with Juan, he knew that it was just a matter of time before he'd be on top.

Anxious to get his hands on the two bricks of cocaine, when he stopped for the red traffic light, he checked his watch for the time. Forty-five minutes had passed. It was almost time to meet Juan, so he made a U-turn and began heading back.

* * * * *

An hour later, Juan parked the tan 430 Lexus in front of the house and pressed the button on his key ring, popping the trunk.

It was beginning to look like a good day. After skinning the dice game earlier for $5,000, and then, making a profitable deal with Ghost, he felt confident things were only going to get better.

Just as he grabbed the shopping bag with the two kilos of cocaine out of the trunk, he noticed a car pulling up behind him. Turning around to see who it was, he was surprised to see that it was Rasco.

It made him nervous so he decided to leave the bag in the trunk and act like he was searching for something else. "Damn …" he mumbled out loud so Rasco could hear him. "That shit ain't in here."

Rasco laughed a cold hard laugh, then pulled a Glock-40 from under his jacket. "Nigga, stop fakin', I know what you got in there … Pull that bag out and set it on the ground."

Juan was stuck. He knew there wasn't anything he could do. Rasco had him. He pulled the bag out of the trunk, slowly placing it on the ground. "All this over a dice game and a few dollars, man!"

"N'all, this ain't got shit to do with a fuckin' dice game. I could care less about that little money. This is about opportunity, and the power of capitalizing on it." He raised the gun up to Juan's face, holding it right between his eyes. "Let me see, how you say it in Spanish … hasta luego!"

Juan took a deep breath and closed his eyes.

Rasco bit down on his lip and he pulled the trigger.

BOOM! BOOM!

Juan felt his soul leaving him when he heard the shots, but then he opened his eyes and couldn't believe he was still alive. Rasco's body dropped right in front of him.

For a second, he didn't know what happened, then he seen that the person standing there holding a smoking nickel-plated 1.45

was none other than Ghost. Blood and brain matter was splattered all over his face.

"Oh my God! Nigga, where did you come from?"

Wiping the blood away with the bottom of his shirt, he said, "I was coming up the street when I seen that nigga had you hemmed up with a gun on you. I already knew what was up, so I parked my car down there ..." he pointed, "and crept around to the back of the house, so he wouldn't see me ... I figured it wasn't no sense in trying to reason with him, so I just ran up and shot him."

"Good looking, my nigga! You was right on time!" Juan said seriously, still not believing what just happened. "Dawg, you saved my life ... That fool had the drop on me, I ain't goin' lie ..."

"Well, at least now you know you can trust me."

Juan shook his head. "You got that right." He agreed. His heart was exploding, thumping hard through his chest as he picked up the bag and handed it to him. "Two keys, just like we talked about."

Ghost took the bag. "I won't let you down, bro."

He nodded, looking him in his eyes. At that point, he didn't give a shit if he did or not, he was just happy to be alive, but just to show he was listening, he said, "I know you won't ... Now, go make us some money while I clean this mess up."

Ghost turned around and walked up the street carrying the bag by the straps, heading back to his car.

Juan watched him toss it in the back seat, get in, then drive away. He looked down at Rasco's slumped body lying in the street, and exhaled. "Damn ... that was close."

Months Later ...

Traverse City turned out to be a gold mine. After getting those two bricks from Juan, Ghost hit the ground running. He rented a small apartment to stash his product – a two-bedroom on the second floor of a three-story brick building, then went straight to work. He set up shop right down the block from the nearest college, where its students loved getting high and partying on a regular basis. He recruited some soldiers and put them in charge of all the daily operations.

Then, once every week, he took a trip back to Detroit to re-up on product, always copping more than before. Juan couldn't be more proud of him. He was handling his business.

By the end of the summer, they were making more than three hundred and fifty thousand dollars a week out there.

Every now and then, Ghost would invite Juan up from Detroit to view the city and have a good time. They would hang out all week, shopping, going to nightclubs, and chilling with different females.

The two of them were nearly inseparable. Whenever you saw one of them, there was a good chance that the other was somewhere close by.

Later that year, Juan struck a major distribution deal with Cholo Dominguez, boss of the most notorious Colombian drug cartel in the entire Midwest. Cholo started selling him kilos dirt cheap, and he, his sister Ayana, Ghost, and all of their soldiers got organized, and immediately took over the streets of Detroit, sewing up every hood.

They were making so much money, they didn't even know what to do with it. Juan and Cholo partnered up and built a real estate incorporation, while Ghost and Ayana maintained control of the streets.

Everything seemed to be going perfect. But nothing could prepare them for what was about to unfold. They didn't know what was about to hit them!

Andolian Napraja

Chapter Two
Spring-2014

Detective Ramone Brown slid open the patio door of his girlfriend's 3,200square-foot central air-conditioned home and stepped outside, letting the impetuosity of an early morning enfold him.

Scented flowers romanced the air, but without knowledge of horticulture, he solely noted the gratifying aroma in passing as he sipped a glass of iced tea and studied the groups of clouds hazily floating overhead.

It was understandable how someone could appreciate such things, Ramone thought, as he glanced around the lush little garden in the well-manicured and very secluded backyard enclosed by an eight-foot high cinder-block wall. He turned around to see Claudia Remirez, his girlfriend of 6 months, still on a phone call in the kitchen, her posture relaxed as she stood holding the receiver.

Claudia was a magnificent hostess who had done nothing to make her seven-year-older African-American boyfriend quest feel unwelcome or uncomfortable, but Ramone couldn't help but to feel like he was an interloper. What made it worse was that he had no clue as to why he felt this way.

In spite of himself, he smiled. Claudia was full of the usual conversation rich people tell each other with hands held high in the air, and it was elating to listen to her entertaining and embroidered stories. The woman had over fifteen years of exploits in high-end real estate. First as a Realtor and Senior Broker for Millennium Real Estate International, then as director of the national branch.

Ramone recalled dining one night with the MREI director, a wonderful memory of a leather-trimmed yacht club in the Gross Point area of Michigan. It had been an unforgettable evening of swapped stories of mansions, private lots and helicopters, topped with champagne and cigars before Claudia dropped him off at home.

But this wasn't the same. Maybe it was all the plaques and photos on the walls outlining Claudia's apparently happy years as a real estate elite that made Ramone so uncomfortable. Or perhaps what was so unsettling was the clear impression that there had never been a time in the past thirty-six years of her life that director Claudia Remirez had ever doubted her abilities. She was only thirty-six and running nearly a third of the country's high-end real estate market.

That was the thing that ate at Ramone the most, how could someone so young be so much more successful than him? Her world was a lot different from the one he came from. The people he knew didn't wake up in the morning and swim thirty laps in a swimming pool to start their day. They had coffee, ate leftovers for breakfast, and read yesterday's newspaper.

"Sorry to keep you waiting so long." Claudia waltzed onto the patio to join Ramone wearing a baby blue bathrobe and house shoes, the sunlight glittering off the crease in her breast. Noticing the strange look on Ramone's face, she said, "What's wrong?"

Ramone grabbed her by the waist, caressing her backside. He thought about untying the robe and fucking her right there, but he was on-duty. "Nothing. Just thinking that's all."

"About what?"

He wanted to be honest with her, but didn't know exactly how to put it in words, so instead he lied. "Just going over some of the details concerning a recent homicide."

"Oh, I see. Anything I can help you with?"

"No, not really."

His cell, phone started ringing, interrupting them. He held up a finger. "Excuse me," he told her as he answered it.

Claudia watched it happen. He went straight into police mode, writing down information on his miniature notebook.

"All right. I'm on my way." Clicking the phone off, he turned to her. "I'm sorry, I have to go. Another homicide. They just found a female in the basement of an apartment building with a gunshot wound to the head."

Claudia let out a sigh. "But it seems like you just got here. Oh, Ramone, I didn't mean for that can to take so long, but you know how aggressive business can he."

He shook his head. "Don't worry about it. I'll see you tonight." He gave her a warm passionate kiss goodbye and walked away, leaving her on the patio.

Ramone's black-on-black Shelby Mustang GT500 was parked out front, gleaming. He pressed down on the remote control starter and the car came alive. He hopped in and raced away with his emergency lights and siren on.

Moving in and out of traffic, Ramone's thoughts were still on Claudia. His instincts were trying to tell him something, but he just couldn't figure it out. He thought about everything that happened over the last few months and tried hard to draw some type of conclusion, but from what he could put together, there wasn't anything that stood out.

"What is it?" He asked himself, beating on the steering-wheel. The car was silent, other than the rumbling vibration of the engine.

Lakewood Manor sat on Fort St., about a block and a half from the red-painted supermarket, not far from the expressway. A modern building with a small courtyard out back, which Ramone remembered from a previous homicide a few years back involving a Hispanic woman stabbed to death by her boyfriend.

The entire block was cut off with cruisers, unmarked cop cars, an ambulance, and lab tech vehicles. A crowd of neighbors, nosy civilians, and thugs mingled across the street trying to catch a glimpse of someone else's misfortune.

Ramone pulled the Shelby in behind a squad car and got out, trudging toward the action, passing a cart of Styrofoam cups filled with coffee. He was met at the door of the building by a short white uniformed officer with reddish-blond hair. The uniform cop blinked twice, then recognized Ramone, who was giving him a cold glare.

"Oh, sorry, Detective Brown. I didn't realize it was you." He stepped aside and let him pass.

Ramone got right down to business. "Where our DB?"

"This way."

They traveled down a hall that lead them to the narrow back stairway. Boots and hard bottom shoes echoed the sound of clucking against the steel-paneled surface as they made their way down. The air was hot, slapping Ramone in the face. No deteriorating smell of any kind, except the stank of old floor lockers.

Lab technicians canvassed the scene, hovering over a young Hispanic woman lying on the floor in the fetal position.

Pulling out a small tape recorder, Ramone scanned the room for clues. The walls had been painted maroon, with bright purple lighting providing a glowing, fun-type illumination. A lot of space from what he could see. The room was pretty open.

He examined the body. Eyes wide, mouth open, rivulets of blood dripping down the left temple. The young woman had taken hits to her head, left arm, left shoulder. She looked extremely attractive and well-kept. Her hair was long with thick curls down the ends. Manicured fingertips on the hand Ramone could see. New designer clothes, expensive stiletto heels. Wait a minute. For a second, one long second, Ramone felt his body go numb. He squatted lower and pulled the woman's hair over her ear, getting a better look at her face. Then a chill hit him. "OH MY GOD... SHE'S A... A COP!"

"What?" The reddish-hair officer said.

"She's one of us!" Ramone shouted. "I know her from around the department. Her name is Sintana Juarez. Detroit Central Narcotics Division."

"Are you sure?"

"Run it. Run her fuckin' name, goddammit!"

The officer did as he was told, contacting the station. A few minutes later, he turned back to Ramone and said, "You're right. Detective Sintana Juarez."

"Where did she live?"

"This address. Apartment number six-o-two."

Ramone stood over her soulless body, his thoughts were nomadic. Who in the hell did this to you, Sintana? And why?"

Andolian Napraja

Chapter Three

His living-space was an ordinary size, with a section of white and black Rent A Center-type of furnishings, no carpet, and three coordinated wooden tables. Many images of The Virgin Mary were placed along the walls and fireplace, with an altar of over one hundred candles and several offering cups smothering the entire dining-room. It always amazed Ramone how Latin people were so invested in their religion.

Emperor Juarez was Detective Sintana's only listed relative in Detroit. He had a round russet face and scudded eyes that almost looked slanted at first sight, but were actually very acute. He wore a blue, red and white zipped-up hooded sweater over a pair of New Era jeans, and white-on-white Nike Air Force Ones. A wooden rosary hung around his neck and dangled from side to side as he sat on the sofa leaning forward, his forearms resting on his knees.

On the grand audio system, Sonny Rich's underground track, "How You Wanna Play It..." vaguely came out the speakers in the background, giving the room a sort of gangster-fied aura.

Emperor kept his attention drawn on the detective, and though he seemed to be well-discipline and intelligent, his eyes were blazing with absolute fury.

Ramone ignored the flare in them and stuck to protocol. "And you say that you two moved to Detroit from Miami?" he asked, holding a pen and miniature notepad.

"Yeah, she wanted to live somewhere where the weather was different from Florida, so she got transferred here."

"And you decided to move with up here with her?"

"I was getting into all type of trouble when I was younger. Sintana used to look out for me. We were always close, so when she told me that she was moving to Michigan, I told her I was coming with her."

Ramone nodded while jotting in the notepad.

"What do you think happened?" Emperor held back on the tears that were starting to boil in the corners of his eyes. "Who did this to her?"

Ramone wanted to reach out to embrace the young guy, but he tried not to get emotionally involved in his cases, even if it was a fellow cop who was murdered.

"We don't know yet, but we're doing everything we can to find out."

"Just be honest with me, do you think it was the guy on the case she was working? You know who I'm talking about, what's his name?"

"You mean Juan Azaria?" Ramone said, shocked that he knew about the case. "She told you about him?"

"Like I told you, me and my sister was close, she told me just about everything. So was it him? Did he do it?"

Ramone let out deep breath. "Well, right now, we don't have any suspects, but you can believe we're checking all angles."

Emperor was quiet for a minute, his eyes looking past Ramone, staring beyond.

"How much did she tell you about Juan Azaria? Did she tell you what her assignment was?"

"No. She didn't say much about it, only that she was working undercover. I told her I thought it was a bad idea, that it was too dangerous. But she didn't listen to me..."

"Is there anything else you can tell me? Who might of had a grudge against her? Someone maybe in her old case files?"

Emperor shrugged. "Sintana didn't have no enemies. She didn't really work too many individual cases like that. Most of the cases she worked were done in raid teams. Nobody would remember her like that."

"What about old boyfriends?"

"She hadn't had a consistent boyfriend since we left Miami. She dated here and there, but nothing serious."

Ramone flipped his notepad closed as he stood up. "Well, if you think of anything, here's my card. Call me anytime."

"Oh, detective. Just one last thing. By any chance, when Sintana's body was discovered, did she have a ring on her finger?"

"No. I'm sure they would have bagged it with the rest of her property. She must not have been wearing it. What does it look like?"

"It was a canary-yellow princess-cut diamond cloaked into a platinum band. She never took it off for anything."

That made Ramone think the motive could possibly be robbery. Something he was definitely going to look into. "I'll add that to the report, just in case something comes up."

"Thanks."

Ramone extended his hand and Emperor shook it. "One again, I'm sorry for your loss."

As soon as the detective left, Emperor started pacing the floor. His expression had turned into a cold piece of stone. He swallowed hard and continued to walk off his frustration and grief. He wanted so badly to kill somebody, but who? He didn't have a clue who was responsible for his sister's murder. The only name that kept popping in his head was Juan Azaria and his supposed-to-be-lunatic sister Ayana.

He massaged his face with his left hand, walking to the front window and back to the altar in the dining-room. He had to find out what Juan and Ayana knew about her death, but how was he going to get close to them? He didn't know them, or even how to find them.

Emperor cursed his sister for not listening to him. He knew she was playing with fire, going in as an undercover cop and playing with a nigga's emotions. You don't do shit like that.

But right or wrong, she was his older sister and no matter what she did, he was always on her side. So if this Juan Azaria, or whatever his name was, had something to do with her death, then he was going to pay with his blood. That he swore. "I don't give a fuck who he suppose to be... "How you wanna play it, hands up, tools out, y'all know what I'm talkin' bout..." he said, quoting Sonny Rich's lyrics from the song he was listening to on the radio.

A plan was forming. He picked up the phone and dialed a number, then paused in the middle of the room waiting patiently for the person on the other end to answer.

*****

Mercedes stood at the foot of the bar impatiently waiting for her pickup tray in her tight-fitting leather outfit that gave away all her pleasurable attributes. Her hair was long and Indian-straight with a part in the middle of her scalp and it seemed to float when she walked, swinging her wide hips through the strip club. "Damn, Coco," she said, smacking on a piece of bubble-gum. "What you doin', girl? I need that drink for my table so I can go."

"Hold on, Mercedes, give me a second. You see I'm working, girl," Coco threw a grin her way. "Just go do your thing, and when you get back your tray'll be ready."

"Fuck that, I need it now."

"All right, ma. Here's your tray, damn. Calm down," Coco said, placing three drinks on her carrying tray for her.

Mercedes lifted the tray over her shoulder, carrying it to her waiting customer. She sat the drink on his table and he grabbed her by the arm.

"Mercedes, you killin' it tonight, baby," he said licking his lips at her, while reaching around and feeling on her exposed ass cheeks.

She giggled, enjoying the attention. "You like this, huh?" She rubbed her hand seductively over her thighs, then grabbed her breast. Smoke always tipped her good, just because he liked her, so she made more than an effort to treat him like a king whenever he came in.

"Hell yeah. We should go and hang out somewhere when you get off work and do something, you know, just kick it. What you think?" he said, squeezing on her butt real tight, then letting go.

"I wish I could, Smoke, but I have a lot going on right now. Maybe we can get together another time or something." Mercedes tried to say it as polite as she could, because she did like him, but the fact of the matter was she just didn't have room in her life for a man.

Smoke was beyond cute, he was fine, and he knew how to treat a lady too. He didn't do or say all the nasty stuff that other guys did and said. He was always nice and she liked that about him. Sure, at times he was extremely flirtatious and could be very touchy, but he never disrespected her.

Mercedes sucked her teeth and batted her eyelashes at him playfully. "I'm so sorry, Smoke."

He downed his drink, then stood up and kissed her on the side of her face. "Don't worry about it, baby. I understand." He went in his pocket and pulled out a roll of money, then handed her several bills. "Take care."

Smoke took one last look at her, then walked away.

Mercedes looked at the money as if it wasn't real. Without counting it, she know he had given her over five hundred dollars, and for nothing. Who does that? She just stared at the money for a moment and thought to herself, where did this guy come from? Maybe the next time he comes in, I'll give him a chance...

But she would never see Smoke again.

*****

It was raining outside. He pulled out of the parking lot of the club in his silver Denali truck and cruised away. A storm had ushered in an early nightfall, desolate and protracted, and he had the headlights on all the way home.

Though tuned to the highest speed, the windshield wipers could barely cope with the cataracts that poured out of the draining sky.

Either the latest drought during this rainy season or Mother Nature was playing a truculent game with the weather. Intersections were flooded. Gutters overflowed.

The Denali tossed wings of water as it passed through one deep puddle after another. Out of the murky mist, the headlights of oncoming cars swam at them like the searching lights of bathyscaphes probing beneath sea trenches.

As Smoke glanced out the side of the window through the plumes of tire spray, his cell phone started ringing. He looked at the display and recognized the name and number on it. "Emperor, my nigga, what it is?" he said answering.

"SMOKE," he screamed through the receiver frantically, "MAN, SOMEBODY KILLED SINTINA!"

"What!" Smoke said, lowering the volume on his phone.

"She's dead. Somebody shot her in the head..."

"Hold on, Emp, slow down. What happened?"

There was a silent pause, then, "I don't know... some detective just showed up and said they found her dead in the basement of her building with a bullet in her head."

Smoke couldn't believe what he was hearing.

"I need your help, bro. I know you're all the way down in Miami, but I didn't know who else to call... I need to find who did this to her...."

"We're like family, Emp, and Sintana was like my sister... Ain't no way I'm going to let you go at this alone. I got your back. Just give me till morning, and I'll catch an early flight to Detroit. Then we can find out what's going on and who killed our sister."

"All right," Emperor said, relieved. "Call me when your plane lands and I'll pick you up at the airport."

"I got you."

"No doubt."

The line went dead, and like the raging downpour of rain had snapped him hack into the full spectrum of reality, he was brusquely deluged by the sounds of the storm, which he had nearly gone unaware of while speaking to Emperor. He had been intently listening to every detail, every word, trying to paint a picture of the situation, only to find that there wasn't much to go on.

Now as the wind's chattered moaning, the thundering rain, the bony squeaking of the wipers scraping against the windshield, and other less-identifiable noises over-flooded him, his best friend needed him, and at that moment, nothing else in the world mattered.

Andolian Napraja

Chapter Four

"This morning a young Hispanic female narcotics officer was found dead in the basement of an apartment building with a single gunshot wound to the head in southwest Detroit ... Fellow officers have identified her as 27-year-old Sintana Juarez, of Detroit's Central Narcotics Division. Our sources tells us that her body was discovered by two teenage boys as they were getting their bikes from storage to go out riding ... Detective Juarez is survived by her brother who lives here in Detroit, and her family in Miami, Florida ... She was a..."

Ayana decreased the volume on the 96-inch plasma screen television with the large square-shaped remote control that had custom high-definition security monitors on it.

She put the remote down on the arm of one of the two sofas, then walked a 180-degree angle around the massive entertainment room in their huge luxurious waterfront mansion.

The 16,500-square-foot estate had magnificent authentic architectural designs that surpassed the other homes in the surrounding community. It had two lavish master suites on the first and second floors, both with water views; a spacious living area with a momentous panoramic display of Lake Michigan, opening into a columned and brick verandah. She and Juan had spent a fortune upgrading its interior and renovating. Everything in the home had been hand-crafted by Spanish designers and tailored to their personalities, right down to the entertainment room where there was a $200,000 surround-sound theater system.

Photos of revolutionary Afro-Colombian leaders and historical military generals graced the walls of every room and hallway throughout the house. They had furniture imported from all over South and Central America to express their individual insights on many cultures and unknown societies.

The game had been good to them. They were making more money than they could spend.

Cholo Dominguez's drug cartel had turned their organization into the number-one supplier of cocaine in the entire Midwest, and they were holding it down.

The butter-soft bronze-complexioned and hazel-eyed Ayana stood in the center of the room, biting her bottom lip with her arms folded, her focus still on the news' latest story - the sudden death of her brother's fiancée, Brazil Sanchez.

In her mind, she thought about the grief her brother was going to feel upon finding out his future wife had been mysteriously murdered. Juan was going to have a fit. Then there was the fact that the girl had been an undercover narcotics officer the entire time.

In any case, she decided she had to be the one to tell him, before he found out some other way. That wouldn't he good.

Hating to be the bearer of bad news, she grumbled under her breath, then called for him. "JUAN!"

It only took a few seconds for him to enter the room clutching a XXL magazine in his hands. "Did you see this article they had in here about French Montana?" he asked. "They say he's the next big thing in rap music... Anyway, why you yelling my name like you're crazy? I was right in the other room."

"I'm sorry, but look at this..." she said seriously. "It's Brazil. She's been murdered."

"What the fuck are you talking about, Ayana?"

She picked up the remote and turned the volume back up. "Listen to this."

"Once again, this morning a young Hispanic female narcotic officer was found dead in the basement of her apartment building with a single gunshot wound to the head …"

"What does this have to do with Brazil?" Juan said, not comprehending.

"Just watch."

He made a "so what" expression with his eyebrows lifted and hands in the air, fingers spread apart.

The reporter continued, "She was identified as 27-year-old Sintana Juarez, of Detroit's Central Division..."

A photo of ,detective Sintana Juarez appeared in the upper-right corner of the screen, and at the sight of her picture, the magazine in Juan's hand fell and hit the floor.

"What the fuck?" he said moving closer to the screen.

Ayana said, "It's her Juan. That's Brazil. She was a cop."

"N'all … I don't believe it. She was ... we were about … to get marr …" Juan took a seat and stared at the TV as if it was something foreign.

The reporter continued. "Detective Juarez was survived by …"

He couldn't take listening to anymore so he clicked the television off and sat there in silence with his arm stretched over the rim of the couch. He felt a pain so deep in his chest he almost couldn't breathe, the emptiness set in rapidly. "I just talked to her last night," he uttered.

He was confused and didn't know if he should he pissed that she had been an undercover cop or angry that someone had killed her. All he knew for sure is that he loved her and no matter what anyone, including his sister, had to say, Brazil had loved him too.

"I know how you felt about her, Juan, but she was a cop. How do you think it was going to end?" Ayana said, trying to bring her brother out the realm of frustration.

He looked up at her but didn't say anything.

"I'll tell you how it would of ended... Both of us was going to be in prison and everything we built over the years and all that we have would of been taken from us. That's what you wanted?"

At that, he searched his sister's eyes for a trace treachery. The hazel in them seemed to have darkened. He gave her a grimacing expression, implying his thoughts.

Ayana knew exactly what he was thinking. "I didn't do it, if that's what you think. She was never that much trouble, and truthfully, I kind of liked her."

"So who did it then?"

"I don't know, maybe somebody from a former case or something? There's no telling who she pissed off, Juan. But we can't worry about that. I hate to say this, but maybe we got a break. Brazil, or whatever her name was, was going to give us up. Ain't no telling how much she already told them."

No matter how much it hurt to admit it, Juan knew his sister was right. Brazil was a cop. She had to be giving them some type of information – that, he knew. "I have... I have to... I have to..." His train of thought had clattered down a slide and chugged to a halt.

I have to what? What do I have to do?

Ayana stood still, allowing him to think. The eerie quietness was more than he wanted. It had substance. The air felt thick with it.

He put one hand to the nape of his neck. His palm was warm and moist. He exhaled.

Outside the window, the night hushed the house as if all of Michigan had been vacated. Darkness revealed itself between the wide louvers of shutters that were ajar. Only the luminance from the table lamp gave the room light.

Instinct was telling him that Brazil's murder was in some way related to him. He didn't know why or how, but he felt it.

He adjusted his posture and surveyed the room with his eyes. Even in the gloom, he could still see her face, as clear as one of the pictures on the wall.

I have to…

The words had been uttered with peculiar tension - and longing.

Now an ominous emotion overcame him, a keen sense of impending danger. It was the premonitory dread that people sometimes felt in their gut.

He hadn't actually experienced anything like it in years, not since the death of his and Ayana's parents, murdered in their home when they were young kids.

Juan had always felt haunted by a malevolent spirit whose premise stiffened the air, making it difficult to breathe, to function, to have faith. As it turned out, his sister had never been threatened by supernatural malevolence or malignancy. The problem had been a treatable mental disorder that frequently occurred during the loss of a family member or loved one. Juan recovered in just a few months.

But he remembered that dreadful feeling too well.

Now he was in its icy grip yet again, though for good reason. Juan and Brazil had been absurdly happy together - considering how she somehow had suddenly appeared in his life.

Nevertheless, Juan knew something was strange about her, but he never questioned her. Maybe for fear of the unknown, he did not know…

He raised up from the couch, went to the window, and opened the shutters all the way. An evergreen tree cast stark, elongated shadows across the acre of land. Beyond those gnarled branches, the beige-brick stucco walls of the guard post next to the house appeared to have soaked up the remaining glow of light; white and gold reflections painted its windows; the place was seemingly silent, and serene.

To the left, he could make out a section of the street. The neighboring homes were further down, about a quarter mile away. Juan had seemed to have forgotten the chaos it took to rule his world.

He closed the shutters, entirely blocking the outside.

Apparently the only danger was in his mind, a figment of the exact active imagination that had made him, at last, an obviously successful drug dealer and businessman.

Yet, his heart was bleeding for the loss of the girl he felt was his soulmate.

Juan, ignoring Ayana's staring, walked out of the entertainment room into the hall, as far as the bottom of the grand staircase. He stood as still as the rail post on which his hand rested.

He wasn't certain what he expected to feel, to think, to remember. The spirit of Brazil, her perfume, her laughter? The restless joking and fun they use to have running through the halls?

Painstakingly, he heard and felt nothing. The grief in his heart grew, his sense of impending anxiety began to overflow.

I have to... I have to... find out who did this to her...

As his thoughts marinated and began to make sense, he found himself caught by floods of memories and started going into a deep trance. He could remember like it was yesterday the smile Brazil had on her face when she received his birthday gift. As he thought of that day, he could feel his mind going back in time to that beautiful moment...

One Month Earlier ...

Yo Gotti's "Cocaine Music" CD blared out the sunroof of the pecan-colored Mercedez-Benz GL550 SUV on 24-inch wood-gold Asanti rims as he parked out front of a little yellow house on the west side of Detroit.

On his wrist was a brown alligator-band and gold puzzle-faced Preguet watch that he had purchased during a recent business trip to Dubai. He tapped his hand against the inside of the door, rhythmically rapping along to the lyrics of the song.

BUMP! BUMP! BUMP!

He blew horn, signaling Ghost, who was inside the house readying a package of money.

When he saw the curtains move back twice, Juan turned to his passenger and she made her move.

She opened her door and some of the most mouth watering eye-catching legs came out, accented with a pair of double short-laced Christian Louis Vuitton stilettos, complemented by soft Tahitian pedicured toes. Her skin glowed with refined felicity, as if God himself was shining his light on her.

Juan watched her stroll up the concrete path that lead to the house's door, her ass firmly plopping underneath the tight-fitting cream full-mini with open-cleavage designer dress.

As she waited for Ghost to open the door, her perfume still lingered in the air inside the truck, hypnotizing Juan.

Ghost opened the door and looked both ways before handing her the bag full of money. "It's all there..." he said, "fifty-thousand. Tell him the rest is still in the safe. I'll move it tomorrow morning. I got a couple moves to make, first."

Brazil grabbed the bag and gave him a warm smile. "I'll be sure to let him know."

She turned around and headed back to the truck.

"Oh," Ghost said, at the last minute, "by the way, happy birthday!"

At that, she laughed. "Thanks."

Brazil climbed back into the truck and tossed the bag onto the back seat and relayed Ghost's message to Juan.

He nodded and stepped on the accelerator, still listening to Yo Gotti spit over the beat.

Brazil turned the music down, then sat sideways in her seat, staring at him. She rolled her eyes when made an irritated expression. "I'll turn it back up in a minute, but first, tell me what you got me for my birthday?"

Juan smirked. "Here we go again! When are you going to learn, Brazil, I ain't telling you shit. You'll see when we get there. Now turn the music back up."

She frowned and sucked her teeth. "You turn it back up. I don't listen to Yo Gotti anyway."

Juan giggled. He knew he had her. She had been trying to find out what the big surprise was all day, but he wasn't giving in.

"It better be good, too. Got me waiting all damn day! This better be one hell of a surprise, I tell you that!" she barked.

He laughed real hard and turned the volume back up.

A few minutes later, Juan was parking the truck in front of a large beauty parlor. "Come on," he instructed.

Brazil smacked her lips, "I don't want to go in." She pouted. "I'll just wait for you here."

"Come on, baby. I promise I'm about to take you to see your surprise, Just go in with me."

She let out a deep sigh of frustration and opened her door. "All right," she whined, "let's go."

Juan held the salon's door open for her and she walked in, rolling her eyes at him. "Make me sick. I can't stand you sometimes."

"SURPRISE!" Everyone caterwauled. "HAPPY BIRTHDAY TOOO YOOU! HAAPPY BIRRTHDAAY TOOO YOOU!" They all chanted the traditional séance, overwhelming her.

"Oh my God, baby!" she said kissing Juan on the lips intoxicatingly.

"You don't have any idea how hard it was keeping this from you. You can be very relentless."

Everybody laughed.

"I'm serious, I thought she was going to kill me if I didn't hurry up and give her her gifts."

She slapped him across the shoulder playfully. "Shut up! I wasn't that bad."

"Umm-hmm, well, take a look around, because this is part one of your gift, so I hope you like it."

Her Face wrinkled. "What?" she said, confused.

"All of this," Juan waved his hands in the air. "The salon, baby. It's yours. I know how you loved styling hair, so I bought it for you... You were so busy pouting you didn't even notice the name on the building outside as we were coming in."

Brazil couldn't believe she missed it. She darted back outside to see the sign.

In big bold lettering, it said "BRAZIL'S HAIR & NAILS BOUTIQUE".

"Oh, Juan! This is... this is... I don't even know what to say." Her eyes started to water. "Nobody has ever done anything like this for me."

Juan wiped the tears away and kissed her on her forehead. "Come on, I want to show you something else."

He grabbed her by the hand and led her over to the attached parking area, and her eyes lit up with excitement when she saw a brand new baby blue Mercedes C300 in the back with a navy ribbon wrapped around it. "Ahhhhh!" she screamed as loud as she could, running towards the car.

"Yeah, who the man, baby! Who's the fuckin' man!"

"You are daddy! You are!"

She got to the driver's side door and realized she didn't have any keys.

Juan laughed, holding them in the air. "Looking for these?"

She sucked her teeth, "Mm-hmm."

He tossed them to her and she couldn't wait to get inside.

"Let's go for a quick ride around the corner and back," he told her.

She put the key in the ignition and listened to the smooth muffle of the engine, gripping the steering wheel before putting it in gear and pulling out of the parking lot.

As they drove past their friends and Juan's family standing in front of the salon, Juan went in the console and removed a small expensive jewelry box.

Brazil felt like she was dreaming. She hit down on her lip like she always did, looking as beautiful as she could be. "Juan, what are you doing? Oh, please tell me you're not about to..."

Juan held up the ring so she could see it. The rock was huge, the biggest she had ever seen in her life. It must of cost a fortune, she thought.

"Brazil Ismarelda Sanchez, will you do me the honor of marrying me?"

Not able to drive, she was forced to pull the Mercedes alongside the curb and think about this. Could she actually he with him, was that what she really wanted? Or was she so deep undercover that her emotions were caught up in the moment. Her mind was telling her to say "no!" and to tell him who she really was, then just walk away, but her heart... her heart was telling her this was right. He was the man of her dreams, no matter what the circumstances were. She looked him in the face, his eyes matching hers. "I... I..." Nothing came out.

Juan reached over and grabbed her shaking left hand, he kissed it. "Just put your heart in my hands, and I'll give you the world. Marry me, Brazil."

Oh, what the hell, she thought, why not? "Okay. I'll do it," she said, making it sound more like a business arrangement than a marriage proposal. "I'll marry you."

"What?" he said, unbelievingly. "Are you sure?"

"Yeah, lets do it, baby. Let's get married."

He slid the ring on her finger and gave her a long passionate kiss. "I'm going to make you a happy woman, Brazil, I swear it," he said, meaning every word.

She hugged her man, squeezing him tightly, tears rolling out the corners of her eyes. "You already have, Juan. You already have..."

Andolian Napraja

Chapter Five

Detroit was awakened by scorching heat and the usual hustling of traffic on a weekday morning during the month of March, temperatures were scheduled to hit the 90s by eleven. By the afternoon, thermometers would be reaching one hundred degrees and rising at roughly the same rate as the tempers of buses, cabs, semi-trucks, and cars commuting through hopelessly bumper-to-bumper packed freeways.

Metro Airport was in a state of meltdown. Overcrowded, overheated, and terribly loud, with no relief in sight from the enormous pressure to add more flights and passengers, and holding the intricate airport operations balanced.

There was no margin for mistakes, and any outside interference could erupt into a cascade of delayed and canceled flights, the result of which would circulate back through the airline system to create gate holds, recesses, and more cancellations across the country.

Crowds of passengers walked by Emperor, exhausted from hours of ongoing delays and waiting, trying desperately to pretend they anywhere else.

Among the melee of passengers with their clunking hags making their way from the sweltering heated terminal, Emperor spotted Smoke wheeling a hand-pulled traveling suitcase, wiping sweat from his forehead with a piece of tissue.

When his eyes met Emperor's, he nodded and said, "It's hotter than Miami up in here! I felt that shit all the way on the plane, and it was air conditioned."

"Yeah, that's Michigan for you. One day it be cold as fuck, and the next day it'd be like this."

Hours of flying on an overheated aircraft had taken a toll on Smoke. He was already exhausted, and now that he had made it to his destination, he planned on resting for a couple hours and catching up on some sleep.

The ride back to Emperor's house was relaxing, just what he needed at the moment. Emperor, knowing he was obviously tired, said very little to him as he drove and allowed him a quantum of solace. He knew how important rest was for the mind, and for what he planned For them to do later on tonight, he knew that it was very much needed.

As he pulled up to his house and parked the car in the driveway, Smoke opened his eyes and looked at the yellow abode, mentally comparing it to houses in Miami. Not bad, he thought, as he got out of the car and stretched his arms in the air, yawning.

When they entered, Emperor showed Smoke to the back room so that he could take a nap, while he began preparing everything for later.

He only owned four guns.

He wasn't a hunter or some sort of collector, but occasionally he did shoot empty beer bottles in the backyard for target practice. Unlike other guys he knew, he never armed himself out of paranoia or fear, he only kept them for the situational need in a world fueled by chaos and confrontation.

He had purchased the weapons, one by one, from dealers on the street's black market, and for a very cheap   price.

In his nightstand, he kept a loaded Glock-21 and a box of bullets. The Glock had light recoil, and stopping power of the .45 auto slug with 10/13 round magazine capacity. Its modular back strap allows for a custom grip based on the shooter's hand size. In case of an emergency, he wanted a gun by his side that was both lightweight and powerful.

Many times before, he and Sintana had gone out to an indoor shooting range, instilling in him a deep respect for the Glock.

Emperor removed the Glock-21 from the night stand and laid it on the bed.

A Ruger 8 762 assault rifle, a NSG pump action with bullpup design 12-gauge shotgun, and another Glock-21 were stored in their original boxes inside a locked wooden cabinet in the dining-room. There were also empty boxes of ammunition in every caliber required.

Though his plan required the use of force, and most importantly, misdirection, throughout his preparation he worried that he was going insane arming himself against an enemy that did not yet exist.

He had no actual proof that Juan or Ayana played any role in his sister's murder. He was simply operating on instinctive insurance, like a soldier thoughtfully constructing fortifications. He had never done anything like this before. By nature, he was a thinker, a planner, and merely a man of action. But this was more like an insured instinctive readiness, and he was captured by it.

Just as he finished loading the weapon in the kitchen, his inner rage was starting to erupt. His patience was wearing thin. He knew he needed to control himself and maintain his discipline, but anticipation was outweighing his equanimity. He felt as if some appalling guilt was bearing down on him, cutting him deep.

Lord help me, he thought - and didn't know if he was asking for protection from unknown enemies or some type of spiritual relief from his dark impulses within.

That night, he and Smoke sat a block down in a stolen Dodge Charger, surveilling a place called "URBAN LEGEND'S DESIGNER CLOTHING & CUSTOM APPAREL." They had learned from asking around in the streets that the store was owned by Ayana Azaria, Juan's sister. Though she didn't actually work there, Emperor thought it'd be a good place to keep an eye on, lust in case she occasionally made an appearance.

Earlier, they went inside to see who was managing it. There were only two guys running the place - a medium-height chubby guy with a bald head, and a taller dude sporting a low haircut that was tapered on the sides and back, with a razor sharp line-up who seemed to he in charge of the store.

He and Smoke had purchased a couple T-shirts, just so they wouldn't appear to be suspicious, and then walked out.

Emperor checked the time on his watch. It was getting late.

"We should go in there and just rob that muthafucka," Smoke said, now wide awake.

Emperor shook his head. "Not yet. We just goin' peep everything out first, then make our move."

"How long you think that's going to take?"

Emperor shrugged. "I don't know, exactly. But when the time is right, we'll know it. Until then, we just have to sit here and wait it out."

Smoke shifted in his seat and got comfortable. The way Emperor was talking, he knew they were going to be there for a while.

Chapter Six

"WHAT IN THE HELL AM I THINKING... I CAN'T MARRY HIM!" Brazil raced home distraught in her new Mercedes, flying down the busy intersection at 65 mph, talking to herself. The marriage acceptance was now daunting her, making her feel as if she had made a terrible mistake. Juan was her target. She had been sent in to win his trust, and eventually, take him down! She wasn't supposed to marry him. It was bad enough that she had been sleeping with him. The department was going to have a fit when they found out she accepted his proposal. What am I going to do? she asked herself.

On one hand, her job was on the line with the possibility of her being prosecuted. If Juan was ever charged, the department would call her in as a witness against both Juan and Ayana, and she would greatly deny everything she had ever told them, which would perjure her under oath.

Then, there was Juan. She wondered how he would react to finding out that, up until recently, she had been posing as a struggling everyday working hair stylist to earn his sister's trust and penetrate his organization; that she was actually an undercover narcotics officer?

Brazil sighed deeply and prayed that all would work out some kind of way,

It was dark and drizzling by the time she made it to her apartment building. She parked the Mercedes out front, behind an older model Ford station wagon. When she got out the car, she trudged across the wet grass toward the large brown door. There was something not right about the scene she was seeing. It took her a minute, then it dawned on her the front stoop light was out. She remembered that Juan had made a point of mentioning it the last time he dropped her off. She had flipped it on that night when she walked in. Brazil never liked to come home to a dark building.

The bulb must have burned out.

She was drenched by the time she got to the stoop. Once under the cover of the small porch, she took a minute to stop and check her surroundings. She didn't see anyone walking anywhere. The block was completely deserted. She figured it was safe.

She fumbled with her keys at the front door. In the dark, it was hard to find the correct one and put it in the keyhole. When she finally did it, it turned and the door opened.

It was pitch black inside. Brazil hesitated. For an instant, she thought she saw something over at the far end of the hall. She strained her eyes and tried to cut through the dense blackness. Nothing. Must have been her imagination. Over the last few weeks, her nerves had been frayed. She and Ayana weren't exactly seeing eye to eye. Ayana was beginning to become jealous of the fact she and Juan had been spending so much time together. Juan was her younger brother and because of that, Ayana felt obligated to protect him.

It had taken Brazil a while to earn Ayana's trust when they first met.

Brazil had real experience with styling hair. She'd gone to school for it and graduated before she even thought of becoming a police officer. When was she was assigned to the Juan Azaria case, she knew she needed a legitimate cover -- one that she could actually be actively working. So she got herself hired as a hair stylist at one of Detroit's top hair salons. She worked there for a month and learned everything about the place, getting her mindset into being an everyday working beautician.

A few days after she was settled in at her new job, the department had told her she could find Juan at Ballers, a night club he owned on the southwest side of the city.

That night, Malana and Chanelle, two of Brazil's co-workers at the salon agreed to hang out with her after they all got off work. Brazil just wanted someone to accompany her so she wouldn't look out of place. Most girls hung out in groups, especially when they went to clubs.

When they arrived at Ballers, it was packed. Music was blasting. Neon lights were flashing in their faces. Girls were dancing erotically in designer dresses with guys in tailor-made suits and expensive hard-bottom shoes. Bottles of Ace of Spade, Cîroc, and Cabana filled the tables with cigars smoking in ashtrays. The club had two levels and a wrap-around balcony overviewing the dance floor.

Brazil spotted an open table and led Malana and Chanelle over to it. The three of them sat down and ordered a few rounds of cranberry-apple vodka on the rocks.

After downing two glasses of vodka, Brazil scoured the place with her eyes, searching for Juan, or maybe Ayana. She had only seen photos of them, so she wasn't sure if she would recognize them in person. She looked over all the faces at the tables close to where they were seated. Nothing. Not even a resemblance. She glanced up at the balcony, searching, but was met only by a disturbing stare from one of the ugliest guys she had ever seen in her life, waving a bottle of champagne at her. Brazil faked a smile and said, "No thanks."

At that, she sighed and mentally prepared herself for a long night.

"You all right, girl?" Malana said, noticing her frustration. "You look like you're expecting to see someone?"

"Umm-hmm," Chanelle chimed in, "I see you were looking around. Who you looking for?"

Brazil chuckled, embarrassed she had been found out, her cover nearly blown. You couldn't pull anything over these girls' eyes, they were up on it. She sat there quietly for a second, trying to figure out a good lie to tell them. "The last time I was here, I accidentally ran into this guy and he was very cute. I just was looking to see if I seen him at any of the tables, but I don't."

Both Malana and Chanelle were staring at her like she was crazy.

Oh God, they don't believe me, Brazil said under breath.

"Well?" Malana finally said.

Brazil shrugged, confused. "Well, what?"

Chanelle giggled. "Well, are you going to tell us what he looks like?"

She and Malana high-fived each other.

"Right," Malana said. "Is he light-skinned, dark, white, what does he look like?"

"Oh!" Brazil said, glad that they had bought the lie. "My fault. Hell, I only seen him for a second. We didn't even have a chance to talk, he was so much in a rush. But he was definitely light, with straight dark hair - that was nicely cut. He had sharp eyes, a small nose, and some of the sexiest lips you could ever see on a guy."

Chanelle laughed. "For a second, it sounded like you were describing a suspect profile for the police! Until you said what his lips looked like."

"Hell, yeah!" Malana said. "Seems like y'all seen each other for more than a second. You described the shit out of him! And what kind of guy has straight dark hair? What is he, mixed?"

"No," Brazil tittered. "Colombian, I think?"

"How in the hell do you figure he's Colombian?"

"Because I'm Colombian. We have a distinctive look from other Afro-Caribbean Latin people."

"Umm, I still say you seen him for longer than a second," Malana said.

Brazil just shook her head at the girls' bluntness. They were something else! She could see herself actually being friends with these two. They would keep her honest.

She took a deep breath and stood up. "I'm going to the restroom, I'll be back."

"Yeah, right," Chanelle waved her hand. "We know you're going to look for your mystery guy!"

Brazil laughed, and the two girls high-fived each other again.

She got up from the table and headed for the bathroom. Just as she was turning the corner leading down the hall where the restrooms were, she spotted him sitting in a booth in the back of the club with a group of people around him. Oh, he's definitely fine, she thought. Brazil stopped in the center of the dance floor and just stood there, admiring him from a distance. The way he talked, she'd bet he had the smoothest voice she'd ever heard; his eyes, though squinted at the moment, were beautiful, he looked better than she had remembered. The photos that the department had of him did him no justice. In person, he was a lot cuter, more preserved. Brazil almost closed her eyes as she began to visualize herself sitting in the booth with him at that moment, his arm wrapped around her shoulders, signifying she was his girl. Umm-umm-umm… she hummed to herself. What a good looking man!

Suddenly, a hand touched her shoulder.

She turned around, startled, and was shocked to see that it was Ayana, dressed in a purple and blue button-up with collar body-suit. She was staring at her skeptically. "Something you like over there?"

Oh my God! Where in the hell did she come from? she thought, her heart beating fast as hell.

"Just checking out the cute guy over there at that table."

Ayana smirked, "Which one?"

"The guy in the tan suit with the blue tie. Oh, I'm sorry, you two aren't …"

"No, he's my brother..." she said, trying to figure Brazil out, reading her body language.

This girl is making me uncomfortable. She's like a fuckin' hawk!

"So, what brings you out tonight? Celebrating or something?"

My God, she is persistent! "No, just hanging out with a couple of my co-workers."

"Oh, and where are they?"

"They're over there at that table waiting on me to come back from the restroom."

"You and your co-workers, where do you work?"

This bitch is good! The department never told me anything about her being so meticulous. This is crazy! I feel like I'm the suspect.

Brazil took a breath and smiled, "We're hair stylists."

"Really? What salon?"

"Nikki's, over on Grand River and Greenfield."

"Oh, okay," she said, seeming to ease up. "How long you been doing hair?"

"Since I was a little girl."

"You any good?"

"What? Girl, the best!"

"Confidence. I like that. By the way, my name is Ayana."

"I'm Brazil," she said, shaking her hand.

"Hmm, maybe I'll swing by the salon one day soon and check you out. See if you have any real skills. I'm actually looking for someone who really knows how to style my type of hair. This is Detroit, there's not a lot of girls that can do Colombian girls' hair."

"I'm Colombian too, so I know exactly what you mean. But, just come by the shop, and get you together, I promise. Here, take my card."

"Okay, just give me a few days, and I'll call you to set up an appointment," she said.

But she didn't. In fact, she never called.

After a week, Brazil thought she would never show up. But one afternoon, as she was putting the finishing touches on a young girl's hair, Ayana walked through the door with another girl who kind of resembled her.

"Sorry it took me so long to stop by," she said, as she and the girl took a seat in one of the chairs to wait her turn. "I got caught up and wasn't free, until now. Oh, this is my cousin, Carmena."

Brazil nodded at the girl.

"Carmena, this is Brazil," Ayana said, finishing the introduction,

Once she was done with the young girl's hair, Ayana examined her. "Long pressed, nice tight curls. Crispy parted scalp. Okay," she nodded, chewing a piece of gum, "I'm liking it."

The young girl smiled and walked out the salon.

"So, how do you want your hair?"

"I'm going to let you be the artist. Just hook my shit up however you want."

Brazil went right to work. If it was one thing she really knew how to do, it was hair. She took Ayana's hair down with a comb, then brushed it a while before shampooing and rinsing it, while adding conditioner. Once she was done with that, she blow-dried it, and began pressing it with a flat-iron. Then she went around her head with a pair of scissors and cut off all the loose ends. Once she was satisfied that her hair was even all around, she began styling, curling her hair all the way down to the edges, and press-parting her scalp to the side in various ways to insinuate her facial features. When she was done, she sprayed her head with sheen and gave her a mirror to check it out.

Ayana stood up, patting certain areas with her hand, while looking in the mirror. She turned to Carmena, who just sat there quiet the whole time, and asked her what she thought.

Carmena got up from her seat and did a quick inspection around Ayana. Finally, she nodded and said, "Yeah, she killed it. I love it. This girl's got some skills."

"Yeah, I think I love it too," Ayana agreed.

"Thank you!" Brazil said, hugging her.

"No, thank you." She said. "Listen, you should come work for me. I need my own personal stylist. What do you make in here, a couple hundred a week?"

"A little more than that."

"Well, whatever you're making, I'll triple it if you come work for me full time."

"Oh, no I can't quit my job. I have to …"

Ayana waved her hand. "This isn't a job. Girl, this is an insult to your skills. Do you really want to work here for the rest of your life? I'm trying to give you an opportunity to make some good money."

Brazil sighed. "I don't know…"

"Just think about it, Brazil," Carmena chimed in. "You're going to be living a life that most people dream of. Flying around the world. Wearing the nicest clothes. Just doing whatever you want. I'm telling you, it's the life!"

Ayana gave her a devious smile. "I know you want to meet my brother."

Brazil giggled. "Y'all make it sound so good."

Ayana folded her arms. "Look, what do you have to lose?"

"All expenses paid?"

"Yep. You'll even get your own hotel room when we travel so you can have your own space. So, what do you say?"

She finally gave in. "When do I start?"

"How about you just did? Here's a two-thousand dollar advance." She passed her a handful of money. "Get all your stuff. Let's go."

From then on, Brazil had been with them. The department was impressed that she had been able to infiltrate them so easily. They had tried several other times but had failed. The guys they sent in undercover was easily spotted. They weren't street enough to fool either Juan or Ayana. Brazil's plan worked because she understood them more than the department did. Before she became a cop, she dated men like Juan, who were drug dealers. She had a brother that used to be into the street life, so she knew the element, and understood it. The department didn't. They identified everything with the application of textbook tactics, with no experience with real criminal culture at all.

The second Ayana introduce Brazil to Juan as her personal stylist at their mansion in East Point, she and Juan instantly became inseparable.

Brazil remembered he asked her to accompany him on the terrace and they sat and talked all night, and in some instances, dreamed together. It was like a fairy tale. Brazil knew she was in trouble the moment she saw him in the club. It was something about him that resonated with her, a distinction she never felt before. It just happened. He made the juices between her legs flow.

Now, as she stood in the doorway of her building, a warm smile crossed her lips in the darkness, and suddenly, she felt more at ease.

She tried to get beyond the entry to close the door behind her, and her feet hit some kind of immovable object. She fell down hard on the tiled floor.

OOUCH!!

Something rugged had scraped against her knee. She felt searing pain as she lay there cradling the wounded area with her hand. The wind from the open door blew up her skirt. Trembling on the floor, she bent over to examine herself, her feet pointing towards the open door. It was then that she became aware of the shadowy figure standing on the stoop in front of her.

Chapter Seven

Ayana grabbed the keys to the burnt-orange convertible
Audi R8 Spyder off the kitchen pegboard. She and Carmena
stepped into the garage. She locked the door to the house, pressed
the button to raise the automatic garage door. Her awareness was at
its peak and harrowing on the thrill of paranoia.

She was convinced that she and Juan were being hunted by
an unknown adversary. The murder of Brazil was proof. Someone
was trying to send them a message.

She could feel her enemy's uncanny presence... a violent
cunning presence that was conscious of her, watching her, probing.
She felt as if a viscous fluid was squirting into her skull under
massive pressure, compressing her brain, squeezing consciousness
out of her. She suffered from grim sensitivity to nearly every one
of her senses; the squeaking clatter of the rising garage door was
ear-splitting; even the distant light of the moon hovering over them
in the sky seemed to agitate her; and a disgusting odor --usually
too faint to be detected attacked like a poisonous mist of vapors
somewhere in the rear of the garage, so potent that it made her
want to vomit.

In an instant, the assault vanished, and she was back in full
swing. Though it seemed like her skull would explode, the internal
pressure subdued as relenting as it had appeared, and she was no
longer on the edge. The tenseness in her joints and muscles was

now gone, and she welcomed the glow of the moon. It was like snapping out of a bad dream -- except she was awake.

Ayana leaned against the Audi. She was hesitant to believe that the worst had passed, waiting tensely for another inexplicable episode of terror to assault her.

Carmena was oblivious to what her cousin was going through, she unknowingly got into the car's passenger seat and shut the door.

Hearing the sound of Carmena's door shutting, Ayana began to focus on her present agenda. She got in the car and started the engine. With weary contemplation, she backed out of the garage and into the street, handling the wheel as smooth as a taxi driver, acutely aware of every neighborhood block.

All the way to Urban Legend's clothing store, Ayana thought about Juan and Brazil, and how happy they had been together. She believed in a world beyond death where eventually she might be reunited with her parents and those she loved. Life was so precious that even a promise of euphoric afterlife wouldn't compensate for the hurt she felt in her heart for those who had died or been killed.

Since they both could remember, they had been down for each other, like Tommy and Sincere in the movie "Belly," coming up as kids running the streets of Miami, robbing, stealing, and even killing, all to establish themselves in the game.

They had made names for themselves, not because the moves they made were all successful, but because they had a knack for making people remember their triumphs and forget any of their failures. That, and the fact they had enough balls to go after drug cartel members and knock them off to take their turf. By the time they were eighteen, every cartel in Miami was after them.

A war broke out and the cartels went after their families, killing innocent women and children to send messages.

They struck back, but were stagnated when they ran out of soldiers who were crazy enough to back them against the cartels. The death toll had reached over forty. Emperor and Smoke were forced to disappear. Emperor fled to Detroit with Sintana, while Smoke hid out in New York for a couple years, then came back when the cartels started to dismantle, due to President Bush's War on Drugs. The cartel bosses had so many legal problems that they weren't thinking about him and Emperor anymore.

In the end, the two cohorts had become legends as being some of the only guys ever to survive a feud with the cartels.

This time wasn't going to be any different. If they didn't get the answers they were seeking, Emperor planned to leave a blood trail all the way back to Colombia, if necessary, until he found the person responsible for Sintana's death.

He and Smoke had been watching the clothing store all evening long, waiting for some kind of sign that would lead them somewhere. They watched car after car come and go. One thing they knew for sure was that there was definitely something else going on inside the store, besides the selling or clothing. There was something illegal going on inside. All the store's clientele seemed to be big-time gangsters or some kind of well-known crime figure. What was the odds of that? Smoke concluded that the store had to be some type of drop-off spot for money, or perhaps, a place for cocaine distribution. Either way they both concluded that whatever was in there had to be of significant value.

"So what do you think we should do?" Smoke said, blowing weed out his nose. He passed the blunt of Kush to Emperor.

Emperor puffed it a few times, then inhaled it real hard, holding the smoke in his lungs to increase the high. "Shit," he said still holding his breath, "somebody has to come pick the money up, so we just goin' wait until they show up."

"How you know they haven't already? I mean, we just seen how many cars come and go?"

"I got this feeling we ain't missed shit. I recognized a lot of the niggas, and none of them deal with Juan or Ayana directly, or they wouldn't be coming here. Trust me, I'll know when we got something." He passed the blunt back to Smoke. "Just be patient a little longer. We'll get them." he assured him.

Ayana and Carmena pulled up in front of Urban Legend's and got out the car. Fat Al, one of her soldiers was standing by the door, he opened it for her. She and Carmena walked in, Rocko was standing behind the counter wrapping up an important business call. Ayana nodded at him and he hung up the phone.

"It's in the back," he said.

She looked at him with stern eyes. "Well, go get it and put it in the car. Fat Al, make sure you keep an eye on the door. Nobody comes in," she instructed.

Fat Al said, "No problem."

Rocko smirked. He loved that she was always all business. There was no playing with her.

He led her and Carmena to the back of the store where there was a slew of boxes that had all sorts of clothing and shoes in all sizes and styles all around the storage room. In the right corner, two big black military duffel bags were on the floor. Rocko picked them up, tossing one over his shoulder, clutching the other in his hand. Ayana kept her eyes on him the entire time, burning a hole in his back with her glaring. She stepped out of the way and let him pass. He carried both bags out to the car with her right on his heels. She opened the trunk and he put the bags inside, then close it.

She and Carmena got back in the car without an utter of a word.

Rocko waved at Carmena. "See you later."

She smiled at him as she and Ayana zoomed away in the Audi.

Rocko turned to Fat Al, laughing, and said, "Ayana is one crazy bitch!"

Fat Al said, "Yeah, she don't play."

"You have no idea."

Rick Ross was coming out the radio real low, spitting over "Mafia Music" when Emperor saw a burnt-orange Audi rolle up with two women inside. He and Smoke watched as the girls went in the store, and a minute later, came back with the guy they'd seen inside earlier, carrying two bags, and then load them into the trunk of the car. It all seemed too good to be true.

"See what happens when you wait? Everything just falls into place. Patience is truly a virtue..." He started the Dodge Charger and followed the Audi as sped away, keeping a distance.

*****

"Did you see that nigga Rocko? He was all in my face!" Ayana said, driving up the busy street, her hair blowing in the wind.

Carmena smacked her lips. "Yeah, I seen his ass. He's always like that though. You know he'll try to fuck anything that got a pussy on it."

"Well, he ain't getting none of this," Ayana said strongly.

Carmena burst out laughing.

"What?" Aryana asked, coyly.

"Girl, you are so fuckin' mean! You ain't goin' ever find a man... You always scaring them away."

"Shit, girl, it ain't my fault these niggas don't know how to handle me. I'm too much for these muthafuckas out here. I need a strong-minded nigga in my life that can hold me down, you know."

Carmena just shook her head. Her cousin was crazy.

"You hungry?" Ayana said, changing the subject. She didn't like discussing her love life.

"Yeah, let's stop at Coney Island or something."

A few minutes later, Ayana spotted a Coney Island restaurant coming up on her left. She switched lanes and when it was time, made a sharp turn into the parking lot.

"Smells good. I'm hungry as hell," Carmena said, taking a scent of the restaurant's good chili smelling food.

She and Ayana got out of the car and went in, unaware that their every move was being tracked.

There were only three guys inside the restaurant; a young Chaldean boy about twelve years old, an older Chaldean man sitting near the door at one of the tables smoking a cigarette, and a Chaldean guy behind the glass-protected counter waiting to take their orders.

He gave the girls a warm smile, then suddenly his eyes widened, alarming them.

Ayana spun around to see what was going on. Two masked men were standing there with guns drawn on her and Carmena. "What the fuck?" She reached for her gun.

"I WOULDN'T DO THAT IF I WAS YOU… GET DOWN ON THE GROUND!" one of them barked as he removed the gun from her purse.

She and Carmena did as they were told, slowly kneeling down with their hands up.

The Chaldean guys were quiet, observing everything and thankful the gunmen weren't interested in taking the restaurant's money.

One of the gunmen snatched both girls' purses off the floor, while the other demanded the keys to the Audi.

"Do you know who I am?" Ayana said through clenched teeth. "I'm going to find you, and when I do, it's going to be-"

"BITCH, SHUT THE FUCK UP BEFORE I SLAP YOU IN THAT PRETTY LITTLE FACE OF YOURS WITH THIS MUTHAFUCKIN' GUN!"

He snatched the keys to the Audi out of her hand and he and the other guy ran out of the restaurant, taking off in her car.

"FUCK!" Ayana said, as she got up off the floor, pissed. You motherfuckers haven't gotten away… she swore. I'm going to find you… I'm going to find you if it's the last thing I do…

*****

Emperor parked the Audi behind the Dodge Charger on a residential street. He and Smoke got out and took the bags out of the trunk. They sat them on the ground and unzipped them.

Smoke whistled. "Damn, that's a lot of money."

"Looks like a few hundred-thousand."

Emperor picked up one of the rubber-banded stacks and flipped through the bills, then tossed it back in the bag.

"All right, look through those purses and see if you can find their IDs."

Smoke rambled through the purses one at a time, until he found the girls' IDs and driver's licenses.

"Check this out… Looks like we hit the jackpot."

Emperor took a look. "Ayana and Carmena Azaria," he said, reading their identification.

"That's your girl, ain't it?"

"Yeah, that's her. Come on, let's go."

They threw the bags of money in the backseat of the Dodge Charger, hopped in the car, and sped away.

*****

"I WANT THOSE MOTHERFUCKAS! YOU HEAR ME? FIND THEM!" Ayana yelled at Rocko and Fat Al, hysterical as she climbed in the passenger seat of the black Suburban.

Fat Al hated seeing Ayana pissed. She could be extremely dangerous. He watched her out of the corner of his eye as she waved the gun he'd given her in the air wildly, talking in Spanish.

"YOU HEAR WHAT THE FUCK I SAID?" she grilled him.

"Si, señora, lo comprende."

"Good," she said, satisfied. She turned and looked at Carmena, who was in the backseat with Rocko. "Don't worry, cuz. I'm going to find those bastards! Nobody takes money from me!"

Carmen just stared out the window as if in deep thought.

Rock said, "Ayana, how in the hell are we going to find these guys? We don't even know what they look like…" he reasoned.

She gave him a chilling glare. "That's your job, you stupid piece of shit… Find them. I don't care what you have to do …"

"But Ayana, it's imposs …"

"WHAT THE FUCK I JUST SAY, YOU STUPID SON OF A BITCH!"

The gun came up swift and smooth. BOOM! BOOM!

She shot him twice in the head.

Carmen flinched, but didn't make any sound as Rocko fell sideways against the door, his eyes and mouth still open, blood all over the window and seat.

Ayana then turned her attention to Fat Al. "You've just been promoted. Now find them! Any questions?"

Fat Al nearly pissed his pants. He kept his eyes on the road and assured her, "No, señora. I'll take care of it."

"Good," she said, lowering the gun. "Now take me home."

"Yes, ma'am."

*****

Emperor's plan worked out perfectly. He and Smoke had made it back to the Coney Island just in time to see Ayana and

Carmena get into the black Suburban with the same two guys from the clothing store.

From a distance, he followed them, staying a few cars behind.

The Suburban took the expressway, and a few minutes later, came up in the area of East Point just outside of Detroit.

Emperor knew the area very well.

He continued to tail them all the way to a huge waterfront Colonial-style mansion, where he assumed Ayana and Carmena lived. "Umm-hmm, got you now, baby."

The Suburban slowly pulled through the black iron fence that had a small guard post at its entrance.

"Home, sweet home," Smoke said.

Emperor smiled in the darkness, sitting low in his seat. It won't be long now, he said to himself under his breath. "We know where to find them... Now we can go home."

Andolian Napraja

Chapter Eight

Brazil erupted in a string of curse words when she saw the cat in the doorway on the stoop. Its long and sleek-moving shadow cast by the street lights took a few years off her life.

It meowed in the open doorway, purring, begging, a pitiful cry about the nasty weather.

Brazil let out a sigh of relief, glad that it wasn't something much worse. She looked at the poor little thing. "You scared the shit out of me, you know that?"

The cat looked at her, then moved away, slipping through the door and into the darkness down the hall.

"Fuck."

She reached down with her hand and felt broken glass. Though she couldn't see it, she knew her knee was bleeding, a serrated edge embedded in it.

She rubbed her fingertips softly over the area and the piece of glass fell out. In the dark, she couldn't tell, but there was a warm trickle down her leg to her foot.

Carefully, she stood, one knee bent a little in pain. Then, an inch at a time, dragging her shoes on the floor, first one foot then the other, she made it to the wall. With her hands, she felt around until she found the light switch. She flipped it on. Nothing.

"Shit."

She slid her feet down the dark hallway, the cat meowing somewhere ahead of her with feline cavalcade. At one point, it rubbed against her leg and Brazil shooed it away with her foot. It meowed louder and scurried halfway down the hall on the hardwood floor, galloping like a horse.

Brazil had left the front door open and she could feel the constant breeze down the hall. For some reason, it was a source of relief. The door was open, an easy exit to reach if she needed it.

Every few steps were interrupted by sounds of the floor creaking. She found the stairs and walked up them, climbing six flights until she reached her floor.

Her apartment was directly across from the stairway in the middle of the long hallway. She tangled with her keys until she found the right one and opened her door.

Plunged in darkness, the noise of a slamming door echoed loudly through the empty hall, a phone ringing in one of the apartments. She nearly lost her balance and fell. Brazil was shaking, terrified. For an instant, before all light disappeared, she actually thought she had seen the silhouette of someone moving closer to her. It was scary. Her mind was playing tricks on her.

She listened but didn't hear anything.

It was the darkness fucking with her. It had to be. She should have closed the front door. She could go back down now and do it, but she was relieved to finally be at her apartment. The phone had ceased ringing.

"Where in the hell is the manager? I sure hope he's working on the electricity… It can't be nothing but a fuse blown."

She turned back toward her apartment, the door open. The cat ran past her, rubbing against her one last time, frightening the shit out of her.

"Go. Get!"

She almost went crazy on the poor little thing. Kicking, she slipped on the floor and hit her elbow.

"Ahhh!" she screamed. "Get the hell out of here!"

Ironically, after all that, all the lights came on in the building.

The cat hurried away, going back down the stairs. That's when she saw her standing there on the stairway with Carmena.

"Girl, what the hell?"

Ayana smirked. "Eww, you're lucky the lights came on… I was about to scare the shit out of you."

Brazil exhaled deeply. "Too late. That fuckin' cat's been doing that since I got here."

"Damn, girl," Carmena said.

"What are y'all doing here, anyway?"

"Juan was trying to call you but you didn't answer, so he sent us over here to tell you."

"Tell me what?"

"He wants you to come down to the club. He's got some kind of surprise for everybody and he wants you to be there."

Brazil sighed. "All right, I have to shower and get ready. I just fell and cut myself downstairs."

"Don't worry, girl, we ain't going nowhere. Go ahead and do whatever you have to do."

It always made her nervous when Ayana came over. She had a tendency of looking around and being nosy. Because of her, Brazil arranged her apartment a certain way. She had photos on the wall of her and Emperor and family members to give the apartment a personal touch, but she made sure to get rid of every piece of mail that had the name "Sintana Juarez" on it.

Brazil took a quick look around the living room, searching everything with her eyes to make sure she didn't see anything with her real name on it. She didn't. With hesitation, she said, "Okay, I'll be just a few minutes… There's something to drink in the refrigerator and some chips in the top cabinet, if y'all want something to snack on."

"Umm," Carmena said, heading to the kitchen, "I'll take some of those chips."

Brazil turned and went down the hall into the bathroom. She cut the shower on, muffling her movements, then crept back to see what Ayana was doing.

Ayana placed her jacket on the arm of the couch and slowly made her way over to the mantelpiece. She picked up one of the photos of Brazil that had a younger looking guy in it that looked just like her.

"Who's that?" Carmen asked, coming out of the kitchen holding a bag of sour cream potato chips, crunching on one.

"I don't know… I think they're family. He looks just like her." She showed the photo to Carmena and kept going down the row of photos, searching each one with care and intent interest.

"Yeah, I'd say he's her brother." Carmena placed the picture back where to it was.

Ayana ran her hand along the edge of the mantelpiece and her eyes fell on another picture of Brazil and the same guy in the last photo hugging each other.

"Hmm… he's cute. I like his eyes…" she said, picking the picture up. And then, she saw it. In the background of the photo, behind Brazil and the guy, a framed Cosmetology certificate was hanging on the wall. She read the name on it and smiled deviously. "Sintana Juarez… Hmm, you little devil, you."

"What you say?" Carmena asked her, trying to get a look at the photo.

Ayana gave it to her. "Oh, nothing. Just thinking…" she said, still smiling.

Brazil caught the whole thing, peering around the corner. She turned and went back to the bathroom, taking her shower.

Half an hour later, she came out wearing a black and silver Prada dress and a pair of six-inch calfskin Balenciaga T-strap heels, a platinum 18-karat rose gold Bulgari Catene watch with amethyst, quartz, pink opals, and diamonds. Her engagement ring sat on the finger next to the one that had the ring her mother had given her for her Cosmetology graduation. The three expensive pieces of jewelry had her whole hand looking icy.

"Damn, girl," Carmena said, putting the chips down on the table. "That's a bad ass dress."

Ayana said, "Yeah, that's fly as hell. You make me want to go change."

Brazil laughed. "Juan had this dress made for me, when we were in Paris. It's the only one like it in the world. Prada made it just for me."

Ayana sucked her teeth. "I see I'm going to have to talk to my brother. I told him about spoiling everybody but me," she teased.

"Girl, whatever!" Brazil said, laughing. "All right, we can go. Just let me turn off all the lights."

Ayana and Carmena started heading for the door. Brazil walked around the room, turning off all the lights. As soon as she saw that Ayana wasn't paying attention, she snuck a quick look at the picture of her and Emperor, photographically remembering every detail.

"Come on, girl," Ayana said, turning around to see what she was doing.

Brazil quickly snapped the last light off, darkening the room.

What the fuck did she see? I know it was something… she thought to herself on her way out the door.

Outside, Ayana and Carmena got in Carmena's white Jaguar XJL and Brazil took her Mercedes. The two cars pulled away simultaneously, with Brazil's Mercedes following them.

In the car, Brazil battled through her memory, desperately trying to figure out just what Ayana had seen to put that devious smile on her face. Brazil remembered taking the picture a year ago. She had just been promoted to the narcotic division. Emperor wasn't happy about it though, he kept trying to tell her to turn the promotion down.

What in the hell was it… she couldn't figure it out.

FUCK! I'm just going to have to be on point… she told herself, knowing whatever Ayana had seen couldn't be anything good. Then it hit her… MY CERTIFICATE! THE NAME ON MY CERTIFICATE! SHE KNOWS MY REAL NAME… OH SHIT!

She wanted to turn around right there on the highway and vanish, but it was too late. She had to see it through. She knew Ayana was going to tell Juan that she had been lying to them. She was going to say things that would make her seem like the worst person in the world. Yes, she would do all of that and more, and Juan would listen, too.

What am I going to do?

Chapter Nine

When you first walk inside the club, there is a hostess named Maria Santos, a bony Hispanic chick that looks younger than eighteen, but is actually 23. Her job is to answer the phone and seat customers. When Carmena, Ayana, and Brazil came through the door, she stood up, thinking for a second they were customers. Once she saw that it was them, she sat down and gave them a welcoming smile.

"Hey, girls."

Brazil waved, "Hey, Maria."

She and the girls kept walking.

The club was almost empty, nobody was in there but all of Juan and Ayana's top soldiers, including Ghost, their junior partner, who was sitting at the same table as Juan.

Everybody was wearing suits and dressed formally. The music was turned down to a minimum. The three tables aside from the one Juan and Ghost were sitting at were all empty.

What in the hell is going on in here? Brazil wondered. This don't look right…

Her nerves were killing her. She kept looking over at Ayana, searching for a sign of some kind that she was going to pull some treacherous shit. Ayana was watching her too, but didn't seem to be interested in telling Juan anything.

Juan stood up, wearing a white tailor-made suit with a silky red tie and a neatly folded red handkerchief arranged perfectly on the jacket's upper-pocket. He opened his arms to embrace her.

She hugged him and kissed him lightly on the lips. "Hey, baby, what's going on?" she said, trying not to sound paranoid.

He smiled at her. "Don't worry, everything's fine. Have a seat."

She did as she was told, glancing around the room at all the different faces. Some of them, she recognized. Some, she didn't. It seemed like everyone was seated according to their rank and occupation. The street team all sat at the same table with Tony Scarfo, their superior; Fat Al and his team of soldiers, who were in charge of security, sat at the table in the far right corner; and last, Ayana fell in with her squad of female soldiers, who didn't look like they were up for any games. The girls had extremely firm faces and dark eyes that were cold. They were all business. Brazil wondered if they were a group of female assassins. Carmen sat at the table with her, Juan, and Ghost. That made Brazil think… what's her role?

Everybody was quiet, sitting with patience and immense discipline. Brazil had never seen anything like it before in a criminal organization. It almost scared her. But she relaxed a little, crossing her legs under the table, and leaned her head on Juan's shoulder, though still keeping her eyes on Ayana.

A few minutes later, Brazil couldn't believe her eyes as the notorious cartel boss, Cholo Dominguez himself, and his chief enforcer, the legendary red hair, Claudia Remirez, entered the club's front door, followed by a small army of soldiers and bodyguards.

Oh my God! The department would have a field day if they saw this! Everybody in here would be charged by morning, just for being in the same place at the same time… What the fuck is happening here?

"Que pass, Juanito!" Cholo said, puffing on a cigar.

"Thanks for coming, Cholo. I appreciate it." Juan shook his hand.

"No problem," he said, looking over at Brazil. "And who might you be?"

Before she could answer, Juan said, "This is my fiancée, Brazil."

Cholo took her hand and kissed her knuckles twice. "Tu hermosa, señora."

Brazil blushed. "Gracias, señor."

Ayana smiled and returned a nod, then looked at Claudia. "Hola, Claudia. It's good to see you."

"Likewise, comrade."

Brazil had once read the file on Claudia. She was considered the most dangerous female assassin the department had ever seen. Her skills were impeccable. She had been trained by ex-military personnel in several styles of martial arts and hand-to-hand combat, weapons, and explosives. She was the real deal.

When Cholo Dominguez decided he was going to wash millions of dollars into the real estate business, he sent Claudia to knock off all his competition in the entire state of Michigan. Claudia went haywire. There was a real estate-related murder nearly every three days for a whole year. Over two hundred dead bodies and no arrests. When detectives were finally getting closer to making an arrest, rumor had it that she murdered everybody that was involved with the case and then disappeared into thin air. Nobody had seen or heard from her in years.

Now, here she was in plain sight.

This is big! Brazil felt honored to be in her presence. She had been fascinated by the woman, a fan of her work. You had to give the girl credit, she was good at what she did…

Claudia and Cholo took a seat at the table across from Juan, Brazil, Ghost and Carmena. Their soldiers and bodyguards stood at ease, watching everything around them. You would have thought the United States President was present, the way Cholo's security detailed the club, posted all around like Secret Service.

"So, what's troubling you, my friend?" Cholo started the conversation. "Why have you called me here?"

"Nothing's troubling me. It's just that it's time, Cholo..."

"Time? Time for what?"

"A few years ago, me and you had a talk about change. I told you in that conversation that there was going to come a time that I would be letting my sister take over all operations for me, including my share in Millennium International. This time is now. I'm getting out."

Cholo frowned, "What do you mean, getting out?"

"I'm done. I'm turning all my assets over to Ayana and taking my money and putting it into commercial investments. Ayana will control the entire cocaine operation and what's left of my stake at Millennium International after I leave."

"Which will be how much?"

"The remaining twenty-five percent. I'm cashing in the other half, which you are welcome to buy, if you like."

"At what cost?"

"Twenty-five million. Exactly what it's worth, or I can sell it to someone else."

"Like who?"

"Me," Ayana said. "If you don't want it, I'll buy it myself."

Cholo considered all of this for a minute. He sat there, silent, letting everything marinate in his mind. Then he said, "So, what's your plan? Now that you're out, what are you gonna do?"

"I got some deals lined up in Las Vegas. I'm going into the sports business. This morning, I bought into a multimillion dollar international promotional franchise. We sponsor and promote all professional championship boxing matches and UFC events and tournaments, and we work directly with TV producers who have contracts with Nike, Adidas, Reebok, and Pepsi. There's no telling where we can take this…"

"And because of this, you want out of the business, why? You can still do these things…" Cholo reasoned.

"I know I can, but I don't want to anymore. I want to establish myself as a legitimate businessman before it's too late and I would like to live my life with my fiancée -- who I plan to marry very soon, without having to look over my shoulder all the time because someone is trying to kill me, for who knows what reason…"

Cholo looked over at Claudia. "What do you think?"

She shrugged her shoulders. "Ayana would make a good partner. We've worked with her several times before, she knows the business better than anybody. I think we'll be all right."

Cholo nodded and said, "Then congratulations, Juanito, on your departure. What can I say, besides I wish you well."

"Thank you, Cholo. I appreciate that, coming from you."

"Now, let us all have a drink."

Juan nodded at the bartender. "Bottles of champagne at every table, with glasses."

"Why didn't you tell me?" Brazil asked.

"I wanted it to be a surprise."

"Did Ayana know?"

"I told her a while back. She's been preparing for it over the last month."

So that's why she hasn't said anything to him! She wants everything for herself and knows if she tells Juan about me, it all could change. Juan just may not walk away and hand the business over to her, but since he was getting out, I'm no longer a threat to him, or even her for that matter. Smart. It's a smart move.

Once the waiters and waitresses poured everybody a drink, Cholo stood up and said, "Let's make a toast to Juan and his lovely lady, Brazil. May they live prosperous for one hundred years..."

"One hundred years!" Everyone said, holding their glasses in the air.

*****

Later that night, once Cholo and Claudia were alone in their limousine, leaving the club, he found himself in deep thought. He had to admit, he had never seen this coming. Sure, he remembered talking about it with Juan years ago, but he never thought he would follow through with it. Many people he knew always talked about getting out, but nobody ever did it… He went through that phase himself, but soon realized he didn't have much of a choice. The cocaine business was all he'd ever known.

Claudia sat across from him, staring out the rear window past him into the late night streets. There was no traffic, just a bunch of street lights and moisture from the rain that came down earlier. She sipped a glass of gin, her last one of the night.

"So," she said, "What do you really think about him getting out?"

Cholo smiled. "You know me too well, my dear… Sometimes I fear you can run this thing without me."

"No, Cholo. I don't have the tolerance that you have to deal with certain things… There will be bodies everywhere if everything was always up to me. I admire the way you handle business. It's very diplomatic. I could never do it. That's why you are who you are and I am who I am…"

He nodded understandingly, thinking at the same time. "We need to find out who this girl, Brazil, is… Where did she come from? What type of connections does she have? I believe she is the root of all this mischief…"

"I'll snoop around a little and see what I can find out."

Now a bit satisfied, Cholo relaxed a little and decided to change the subject. "How's everything coming along with your boyfriend?" he said with a chuckle.

"Ha-ha-ha! Ramone's good." She took a sip of her gin, grinning at him over the glass. "I think he's in love. Stupid bastard has no idea who I am... Next week, he wants to travel to Acapulco for the weekend and rent a villa."

"Good. Keep him close. Keep him real close. When the time comes, we'll take him out, and the girl too."

Claudia laughed and said, "With pleasure, Cholo. With pleasure."

Andolian Napraja

Chapter Ten

It was like a fairy-tale. Brazil was so happy that she was actually considering getting out of the police business. With her hair salon, she could live comfortably on her own now and do what she wanted. She couldn't believe that Juan had really quit the game.

In a way, she was proud of him and, at the same time, relieved, because now she didn't have to worry about him going to jail.

The department didn't have anything but circumstantial evidence against him, nothing concrete. No drugs. No informants. No wire taps or surveillance footage. Nothing. Just the little reports she had filled months ago, and they were now all outdated. His organization's tactics always changed, nothing ever stayed the same, which was how he always stayed ahead of authorities. The department had him as a ruthless, psychopathic, homicidal maniac who deals drugs for a living. But the truth was they didn't know Juan the way she did, and the real monster behind his organization was Ayana.

Over the months Brazil had been around them, she had personally witnessed Ayana execute or kill several rival drug dealers, including women. The girl didn't discriminate.

Juan was completely the opposite of his sister, the business mind of the two, having started selling drugs at the age of fourteen, then striking a major distribution deal with Cholo Dominguez's drug cartel by eighteen and becoming a multimillionaire providing the entire midwest region with cocaine. Not to mention that, until recently, he had been the clandestine partner and co-owner of Millennium Real Estate International, and now, a legitimate businessman in the sports promotion industry. Brazil wondered what would he do next? It seemed that he was always elevating to another level, doing things most people couldn't even fathom. And he did it all with ease. It came to him naturally, like a sixth sense. You just never knew with him, anything was possible.

She and Juan had to come back from their vacation in Managua, Nicaragua, because he had to head to Las Vegas to assist his team and partner with the promotion of an upcoming championship fight at the UFC area. He had to leave that night. Brazil spent the next week alone at her apartment, waiting for her man to return.

After he got back, they planned to move in together immediately and, in a couple months, get married. Brazil was already doing her bridal shopping and looking for her wedding dress. Juan called her every night from Las Vegas to make sure she was okay and to hear her voice. It was killing him not to be with her.

*****

Detective Ramone Brown was in his office, working on a recent homicide, when he received an unexpected phone call from Ayana Azaria, asking him to meet that afternoon at Deangelo's, a middle class Italian restaurant in the heart of St. Clair Shores.

Deangelo's was a brick structure comprised with many windows that had a romantic setting, blended with stylish ceiling lighting, exquisite dinners, and fine wines.

When Ramone walked in, he saw that Ayana was already there, seated at a booth to the right, enjoying a steak dinner.

"Welcome to Deangelo's, may I help you, sir?" the lovely Italian hostess said, standing at the podium in front of him.

"Yes. I'm here to see that woman over there," he pointed toward Ayana. "We have an appointment."

"Oh, right this way please. She's been expecting you."

The hostess escorted him over to the table. Ayana stood up and shook his hand.

"Thank you for coming on such short notice."

He smiled and sat down across from Ayana. "It's not that often I get a call from the queen of the city, so I know this is going to be good," he said jokingly.

"Very funny, Ramone." She cut a piece out of her steak and chewed it down with a swig of wine. "Hungry?"

"Not really, but I'll have a drink though."

"Let me guess, Remy, right?"

It never ceased to amaze him, she was always on her game. "You guessed it," he said, shaking his head, wondering how she did that.

Ayana laughed, knowing exactly what he was thinking. She reached across the table and touched his hand with hers. "It's my job, Ramone, to know people. That's how I stay alive in this business."

She waved her hand at one of the waiters and he approached their table, holding a tray in his right hand.

"Yes?" he said.

"Can you please bring my friend a glass of Remy?"

"No problem. Just a second."

"Thank you."

Ramon nodded at the young guy respectfully, and he disappeared through the double-doors into the kitchen.

"I haven't heard from you or Juan in a while… Business must be good, huh?" he fished, trying to figure out why she had called him there.

"Something like that. Patience, Ramone," she said, still reading him. "Wait until he brings your drink, and I'll let you know why I've asked you here."

A few seconds went past, and the waiter came back with a bottle of Remy, a short glass, and a small bucket of ice on his carrying tray. He sat the glass on the table in front of Ramone. "Ice?"

"Yes, thank you."

He scooped a few ice cubes out of the bucket with an ice-scooper and shuffled them into the glass, then poured him a drink.

Ayana sat there quietly, watching Ramone, letting him feel a bit uncomfortable. It tickled her inside. There was nothing like having a cop on your payroll that was afraid of you. It made her pussy quiver knowing that she could crush him at any given time she desired.

She and Ramone shared a confidential relationship that went beyond the borders of his police work. They met a few years back when he was investigating the murder of Mena Azure, her and Juan's aunt who had been stabbed to death by her boyfriend, Carmelo Jackson, a local drug dealer from Southwest Detroit. The incident took place at the same apartment building where Brazil lived, though in its back courtyard. Ramon had been the leading detective on the case was doing check-ups with the Azaria family to see if anyone could provide any information explaining why Carmelo had snapped and killed Mena, which was how he came across Mena's nephew and niece, who turned out to be the infamous Juan and Ayana Azaria. The two notorious siblings that controlled much of the cocaine trade in Detroit.

Months after Mena's death, the case took an unexpected turn when Carmelo, who had been on the run for murder, was found in a back alley, shot to death.

Ramone had his suspicions that both Juan and Ayana played an essential role in Carmelo's murder, but he never filled it in any of his reports, figuring Carmelo got what he deserved for doing what he did to Mena. Juan and Ayana swore to him that neither of them had anything to do with Carmelo's death. Both insisted that someone else had beat them to it, though they were very grateful to the secret assailant for doing them the favor. Ramone kept coming around after that, snooping for more information, until one day Ayana pulled a pistol on him and set him straight, warning him to seek information elsewhere. Ramon took the threat seriously, and since he was in a desperate spot in his life, figured he'd try his luck at offering his assistance at being their personal hired informant, which Ayana couldn't resist. She gave him a list of names of rival real estate developers who were in competition with her brother and Cholo Dominguez at Millennium Real Estate International.

A day went by, then Ramone called her with the addresses and locations for every name on the list. This was the beginning of a business relationship that would last for years to come. Juan and Cholo sent her and Claudia Remirez to wipe out all of their rival competitors, and Millennium Real Estate International became number one in the business all over Michigan. Ramone had made a small fortune working with them, more than he would ever make in his entire career as a police officer.

When the waiter had left, she said, "I need a favor, Ramone. I have a hunch about something... And I need you to see what you can find out."

Ramon took a drink of Remy. "Concerning what, exactly?"

She slid a photo across the table with a name at the bottom of it. Ramon picked it up and read it out loud. "Sintana Juarez. Who is she?"

"That's what I want to know. I want to know who she works for, where she came from, anything you find out."

"How long do I have?"

"I need to know as soon as possible. My brother plans on marrying her soon. I have to know if she can be trusted. She's been going by another name ever since we met her; Brazil Sanchez. I just found out it was an alias. Now I want to know who she really is…"

"I'll work on it right away. Give me until tomorrow morning."

"You got it."

Chapter Eleven

Her hair fell in thick clumps onto the bathroom floor. She took the scissors, cutting again. A new face emerged in the mirror. She said goodbye to the person she had been for the last few years. A new Claudia was born.

From the bathroom, she could hear Ramone unlocking the front door, coming home from work.

"Claudia, you here?"

Oh, was she ready to get rid of him. It was starting to drive her insane, trying to hide the true feeling of hatred she had for his occupation. It's not that Ramone was a bad man, it was just that she despised police and other law enforcement agencies. She hoped Cholo figured it out - what to do with him. She couldn't dare spend another year pretending to be in love with him.

"Claudia?" he called out again.

Irritated, she said, "I'm in here, washing my hair. Be out in a minute."

Claudia stuck her head under the faucet into the running warm water, and rubbed a glob of moisturizing cocoa butter shampoo all over here hair, massaging it into her scalp.

At last, she had reinvented herself. It felt liberating.

Ramon grabbed her from behind. For an instant, she thought his tongue was attempting to invade her mouth, and she began to recoil. Then, she realized that as he kissed her unresponsive lips, he was in fact trying to say something to her.

Under his breath and impaired by the crush of their lips, it sounded like: "I see you…"

Claudia might have resisted, but at the moment she gave in. His lips kissed her closed mouth, and he gave up, figuring she wasn't feeling up to it. He pulled his head away to the side for a long follow up hug that was so tight, it nearly cracked her ribs.

"It's good to see you, baby. Give me a hug."

Claudia didn't realize it, but her arms on his back were as limp as a rag doll. Thankfully, at the moment her facial expression was hidden in his broad shoulder.

Dubiously, she flattened her hands against the girth of his arms and squeezed. He was several inches taller than her, even in heels, and hard as a rock. Though her first reaction was to recoil at the thought of enjoying the moment, she couldn't fully claim that it was totally unpleasant.

"Yeah, that's it," he said, cheerfully. "Come on now, smile."

When he turned and left the bathroom, she flashed a mischievous, wide grin. Claudia's smile was a bewilderment of many conflicting emotions. She felt sick to her stomach and nearly looked it. She ran a towel through her hair, attempting to dry it, as she followed behind him out into the living room, carrying her role as his loving companion. She sat down in one of the two reclining chairs. Ramon dropped into the one next to her, taking her hand in his.

"Claudia, you okay?" he said, concerned. "You look a little… Oh, wait a minute… You cut your hair!"

"Umm-hmm," she mumbled.

He kind of rubbed his hand over her head and touched the ends of her hair. "It's good. I like it…"

Ramone didn't know it, but the entire time he was talking to her, Claudia's eyes were on the photo sitting on the coffee table. She heard his words, though they echoed, but what sent a chill down her spine was that it was a picture of Brazil, Juan's girlfriend. The same girl she was seeking information on.

She decided to play stupid to see how much he knew about her.

"Who's that?"

"What? Who?" Ramon looked straight ahead, trying to see what she was talking about.

"The girl in the photo…"

"Oh, her name is Brazil Sanchez, well at least that's what she's been going by."

"What do you mean?"

"I just got some information today that says she might be a girl named Sintana Juarez. Speaking of which, I need to do a quick search in the department's database to see if I can match her correct name with her face, and maybe find out who she really is."

Claudia nodded, but she couldn't believe how this had fell in her lap. "Why, what did she do?"

It was normal for Ramone to discuss some of his cases with her, so he wasn't the least bit suspicious. "Actually, she hasn't done anything that we know about, but she's been possibly using an alias name, and we don't know why… So far, the department has no interest in her. I'm just doing this for one of my private clients."

She didn't dare try to push him to tell her what client that might be. She didn't need to know, because it didn't matter. She just kept her mouth closed and waited for Ramone to show her everything she needed to know, without her asking.

Ramon went in the bedroom and grabbed his laptop, setting it up on the kitchen table as he always did, and entered first the name: Brazil Sanchez, just to be sure nothing was associated with that name. He waited for a few seconds and a few different girls with the same name popped up, though with different middle names. He scanned each of their photos to see if there was any resemblance to the one he was looking for, but there wasn't any. Neither of the girls had the slightest. Next, he entered the name: Sintana Juarez. It only took a second for her picture to pop up at the top left corner of the screen, and he saw associated with her name shocked him. She was a narcotics officer, and had been for the last four years.

She must be undercover right now, thought... Damn, this isn't good... Fuck!

Claudia saw everything. It took all that she had not to start smiling, but it was killing her inside. The girl was a cop. Who would have ever thought? This was better than she thought.

Umm-umm-um... Just wait until Cholo finds out about this...

Chapter Twelve

There was a disturbing knock at his bedroom door.

It was early in the morning. Emilia, his wife, was still asleep. Groggily, he turned over and blinked at the clock. What the fuck, 7:37 a.m., it's Saturday...

"Yeah, what is it, Julio?" he mumbled.

"Sorry, sir, Ms. Remirez asked me to wake you. She's downstairs in the kitchen. Uh, she says it's very urgent, sir."

"She got something?" A seven-in-the-morning question.

"I don't know, Mr. Dominguez, but I would guess whatever it is, it must be very important to wake you this early."

"It better be."

Ten minutes later - in slacks and a tank-top, and several thoughtful brushes through the hair - he was at the kitchen table, staring Claudia in the face. "Find anything?"

She was an angel of death, dressed in an all black business suit and black coat. "Her name is Sintana Juarez. She's a cop."

"A cop? What do you mean?"

"A cop, Cholo. She's an undercover cop. Juan doesn't even know it."

Julio set a hot cup of coffee on the table in front of Cholo.

Not that he doubted her or anything, but for his own curiosity, he had to ask, "And how do you know this?"

"I don't know who, but someone hired Ramone to investigate her. They found out her real name somehow, and asked him to see what he could find on her. Well, it turned out she's an undercover narcotics officer by the name of Sintana Juarez. And guess who she was assigned to take down."

"Juan and Ayana."

"You got it."

"This is good, Claudia. This is real good."

"I found out last night, but I couldn't get away until this morning."

He sat there for a minute, thinking and sipping from his cup. "Where's Juan at this minute?"

"I hear he's out in Las Vegas promoting a fight, and won't be back for a few days."

"Julio, get my son on the phone. Tell him to come home now."

Claudia said, "You're sending him to handle it? You should let me take care of this one, Cholo."

"No, it's time he proves himself. After all, you trained him."

*****

Ghost woke up to the touch of something warm on his face. It was a warm wash cloth.

It felt good. He sighed as he embraced that slight bit of comfort. He lifted his head a little so he could look around. He was lying face down on a queen-size bed, in a room with bare walls and a single wall-sized window that had long sky blue curtains hanging from it. There were other things in the room, such as a dresser with a huge mirror on top, and a bedside desk with a lamp.

Carmena held out his cell phone in front of him. "Here... Someone named Julio is on the line. I made some breakfast, if you're hungry."

He took the phone. "What time is it?"

"About eight."

"Eight in the morning?"

"Yep."

Why the fuck is this nigga calling me this early?

He wanted for Carmena to leave, then took the call. "Julio, what's going on?"

"Your father wants to see you. He said come home now. It's urgent."

"Everything all right?" he asked, getting dressed, using the hot rag to wipe his face.

"Don't get all worked up, it's business. Nothing's wrong. Just get here as soon as you can."

"Be there in half an hour." He turned the phone off.

Carmen appeared in the doorway. "You gonna eat?"

"N'all, I'm good. I have to go. But I'll see you later on tonight."

She was disappointed, but she could tell from the way he was moving that whatever that call was about, it had to be serious.

He kissed her on the cheek. "See you later." And he was out the door.

*****

Later that day, Brazil stood at one of the windows and watched the gray clouds roll from the west, driven by the wind. As they came, the earth below them darkened, and sun-mantled houses put on cloaks of shadows.

The inner sanctum of her single-room, sixth-floor apartment had two large panes of glass that provided an uninspiring view of the expressway, a shopping center, and the nearly jammed-together rooftops housing tracts that receded across Wayne County, apparently to eternity. She could still be enjoying her panoramic ocean vista or a window on a sandy covered beach-front with her Juan in Managua. But she was stuck in her old stanky apartment all day with nothing to do but daydream about their vacation that ended too soon.

No, she wouldn't think about that. It was more like her to worry about the possibilities instead of the things that were reality.

Live for the moment, Juan would tell her. He was a born therapist. Sometimes, she thought she would learn more from him that from a certified counselor with a doctorate in psychology.

In truth, the constant bustle of the scene beyond the window was invigorating. And whereas she had once been so predisposed to gloom that bad weather could negatively affect her mood, all this time with Juan and his usually smooth persona and positive outlook on life had made it possible for her to see the somber beauty on what felt like a dreadful day.

She and Emperor had been born and raised in a loving home as warm and comforting as a song by Luther Vandross. But those days were long behind her, and the effect of them had long ago diminished.

Live for the moment, Brazil. It's all you got. The moment.

Beneath her window, she stared out into the courtyard and remembered some time ago a young woman was stabbed to death down there. Butchered. She had watched in awe the entire gruesome incident with tight-jaws and clenching teeth as the young woman came from around the corner, running and screaming horrifically, her attacker right behind her, clutching a long, rugged knife. Its blade reflected a purplish shine off the glow of the moon. He grabbed her by the hair, sinking the knife deeply in her shoulder bone. The woman let out a chilling howl, screaming at the top of her lungs.

He launched again, this time somewhere near the center of her back.

"OHH-HO-MY-GOD! SOMEBODY HELP ME, PLEASE!" she cried in agonizing pain, falling to the ground.

The woman turned around, crawling in a backwards position using her hands and feet, never taking her eyes off of him.

He reached out and slashed her across the face.

Blood trickled down her cheekbone and dripped from her chin onto her shirt. Her attacker grunted, making a fist around the handle of the knife, throwing himself on top of her, striking her repeatedly with intrusive force. Spurts of blood rained black drops from the air, painting the ground.

It went on for what had to be a long two minutes. Lash after lash. Brazil could feel the blade going in and out of the woman's body. She wanted to holler, to shout 'STOP IT, YOU SON OF A BITCH! LEAVE HER ALONE! I'M A POLICE OFFICER!'

But she didn't.

The words wouldn't leave her mouth.

All she could do was watch as the poor woman met her deadly fate. It was the most terrifying thing she had ever seen in her whole life, and she would never forget it as long as she lived.

Shook from the grim memory, she reached her hand out to close the drapes and jumped back as she thought she seen a man watching her down in the courtyard. She took another peep and could see him as clear as the sun, a daunting presence, studying her from afar. She squinted her eyes, trying to make out his face, but he backed away from sight to the side of the house.

Once the window was covered, the apartment felt warm and cozy. All thoughts of the stabbing incident and the mysterious stalker outside seemed to have left her, lost in the realms of her mind.

Just as she was starting to relax and listen to Sade's "By Your Side" on her Kenwood stereo system, he cell phone started beeping. She walked over to the table and picked it up, reading the screen. It was a text: BABY, I NEED YOU TO MEET ME DOWNSTAIRS... I'M IN THE BASEMENT... HURRY UP, IT'S IMPORTANT!

JUAN?

She couldn't believe he was back already. She sent him a response: I'M ON MY WAY...

She raced out of her apartment, hurrying to lock her door. She darted down the back staircase, flight after flight in stilettos, moving with urgency. She couldn't wait to see her man so she could hug him and feel his strong embrace around her body. It had been a long wait. All she wanted to do was be with him again; to feel his kisses and gaze into his eyes. She was his and he was hers.

When she came around the last flight of stairs, Ghost stepped out, catching her completely off guard.

WHAT THE FUCK!

With a balled fist, he punched her right in the face between her nose and lips with all his might, sending her towering sideways, falling down the remaining stairs. He was on her, grabbing her from the back by her hair, and dragging her on the floor of the basement. A strange cry escaped her mouth, but not loud enough to alert anyone in her building that she was being attacked. Ghost slapped her again, this time in her chest, knocking the wind out of her. He kicked her ribs with his thick rubber sole Mauri boots, forcing her into the fetal position, then gave her another blow to the jaw, knocking her unconscious.

When she woke up, he was standing over her with a smile on his face, and a gun in his hand equipped with a silent suppressor at the end.

Brazil didn't understand why this was happening to her... Did Juan find out I'm a cop and send this monster son of a bitch to kill me? she asked herself in disbelief. She was defenseless against him, her entire body ached with excruciating pain, and she was sure that her jaw was broken.

She looked into his eyes, and tried to see if the person she had known as a friend was still somewhere behind them, but they were cold and emotionless, black, far from mercy or compassion.

"Ghost... why.. are... are you... doing this?" she uttered through busted lips, the left side of her face swollen from his brutal assault.

Still no leniency, he stood there with a sadistic smirk. "Your boyfriend brought this on you..." he said. "He should know better than anybody that it ain't no getting out this game...."

"But ..."

PUTE!

He sent a direct shot to her temple, silencing her.

She died in the basement of her building feeling like she was being punished for allowing that young woman to die in her courtyard that night. Brazil knew she should have done something, she should have said anything to help her, but she didn't. She just stood there and watched. And now her fate was sealed just as the woman's was. Her only solace came from knowing Juan had nothing to do with it, and that brought her peace in her final breath of life as she faded away.

Ghost removed both rings from her fingers and put them in his pocket. One he would give to Carmena as a gift, to set his next plan in motion. The other one he would pawn for money, just because he didn't have anything else to do with it. Before jogging up the stairs, he took one last look at her, feeling kind of bad, but it had to be done. "So long beautiful." he said, "so long ..."

Andolian Napraja

Chapter Thirteen

Carmena's doorbell rang repeatedly, chime after chime. It took all her strength not to yell "WHO THE FUCK IS IT?"

Instead she said, "Here I come. Hold on!"

She stomped her petite little feet all the way to the front door and flung it open without caring to peep through the hole to see who it was. She was thrilled to see that it was Ghost.

He stood in the doorway laughing. "Girl, who you hollering at like that?"

Her whole expression, attitude, and mood switched instantly from rage to elation. She threw her hands around his neck like she hadn't seen him in days, squeezing him with everything that she had as he cradled her ass with both his hands, kissing her delicately. She couldn't believe he kept his word and came back that night like he said he would.

"Damn, girl, you goin' let me in or are you goin' make me stand out here all night?"

She grinned, looking into his eyes. "Oh, I'm sorry, but I been missing you," She back away to allow him inside. "Where have you been all day? I thought something was wrong, the way you left this morning."

"Well, everything's good. Just had to take care of some business for my family, that's all." He tossed his jacket over the arm of the couch. "So what was your day like?"

"I had to go down to Brazil's salon this morning... You know I been managing it since she was out the country with Juan for their vacation, and although she's back now, it still gives me something to do, We just got some new vendor machines in, I had to be there when they arrived so I can sign for them."

At the mention of Brazil, Ghost remembered he had something to give her. "Oh, I got something for you," he said, smiling.

Carmena looked confused, "What?"

"Just close your eyes, and don't open them until I tell you to."

"Okay, papi," she replied excitedly, shutting her eyes and putting her fingers over the lids, so he'd know she wasn't peeking.

Ghost went in his jacket pocket and pulled out a small black jewelry box he had picked up from the pawn shop after selling Brazil's engagement ring for $10,000.

"Can I open my eyes now:" she asked with a wide smile, bearing all her upper teeth.

"All right, open them."

When she saw the ring sitting in the box, she nearly melted right there. It was the most beautiful ring ever -- a canary yellow diamond on a platinum band. "Oh, Ghost, I love it!" she said, holding her breath.

"Now I don't want you to get the wrong idea or nothing. I'm not asking you to marry me. I'm just letting you know I care about you." He slid it on her finger, a perfect fit.

Carmena felt all mushy inside, she twirled the ring around her finger, then held her hand out looking at it from various angles. Ghost really stepped his game up, she thought. She hadn't seen this coming. Even if it wasn't a marriage proposal, it was a step towards it. Her emotions were so captivated by the sentiment that she couldn't see through the wicked grin on Ghost's face, and the trickery behind his gift. Little did she know, she was a pawn in a deadly game of real life chess.

She wanted to show her appreciation, so she slid her hand down his pants, grabbing his half-erected penis, stroking it gently. Using her tongue, Carmena licked his lip and kissed him tenderly, while massaging his now hardened python. She unzipped his jeans, exposing his stiff protruding member, and flicked her tongue over the dome, licking it with skill and focus. Ghost let out a deep groan, exhaling. She was a pro, with one quick motion she took him all the way down her throat, devouring him, sucking and stroking the shaft with her hand synchronously until his load squirted hot milk all over her uvula. She swallowed every drop like her life depended on it, fervently drinking him.

Ghost looked down at her, his dick still inside her pretty little mouth, and grabbed the back of her head, emptying the rest of himself in her trachea. Now that was worth a dead bitch's ring, he thought, giggling to himself heartlessly. "Haaaah, I love this shit..." he said loud enough for Carmena to hear, and they both started laughing.

Andolian Napraja

Chapter Fourteen

After taking almost $100,000 in cash from Ayana and Carmena, there was no looking back. The two comrades spent the next couple months recruiting workers and soldiers throughout the city to assist them with moving kilos of grade-A heroin and some of the best Colombian cocaine money could buy.

Their team was raw, taking the streets completely by storm, robbing and murdering their competition, and seizing their territories in the end.

In just a couple months, Emperor and Smoke had half of the city of Detroit under their control, making more money than either of them had ever seen in their lives. The whole city was talking about them.

It wasn't uncommon to catch Smoke jumping in or out of one of his many foreign rides with a bad chick by his side on any day of the week,

Emperor was living like a king in a massive and luxurious suburban mansion with eighteen-foot-high cathedral ceilings and ancient Spanish paintings and historical artifacts comprising the walls. He blew everybody's mind when he pulled up on the Belle

Island strip in a new black and silver Rolls Royce Wraith puffing on a Cuvee Cusano cigar, and drinking a bottle of 1849 Francios Rebelious Cognac, with the music cranked all the way up, not giving a fuck.

He and Smoke had become instant celebrities in the hood, and had built a stand-up reputation with everybody who knew them for handling business in the utmost fashion and taking no nonsense.

But the streets were talking, and people were starting to wonder where these two had suddenly appeared from. It seemed like the two of them wanted to draw attention to themselves on purpose, and from all the wrong people too, something the older gangsters and drug dealers didn't understand... Why would some niggas who were getting so much illegal money live so flamboyantly, as if they didn't care about federal indictments? The feds had to be on to them by now, the old timers suspected.

But it didn't even seem like the two of them gave a shit, and that was a red flag to old timers. One older drug dealer named Brazzi, from the west side of Detroit, had tried speaking with Emperor once about his outlandish behavior and lavish spending, warning him that he would eventually attract the wrong attention from local authorities and federal agencies, but Emperor told the old timer he should mind his own business, and further assured him that he had no intentions of going to prison. No, he would hold court in the street, which was why he kept a S8762 assault rifle in his passenger seat at all times, just in case police tried to pull him over, or come after him for any unknown reason. He wasn't going down without a fight.

Something wasn't right about that nigga, Brazzi concluded. How could somebody getting all that paper be so arrogant and stupid, and act like he had a death wish?

It just didn't add up. But he would do as the youngster advised and mind his own business, and just let him do him.

Though he knew from experience, like all the others did, how it was going to end, and it was a shame to see a young nigga with so much potential throw it all away like that, and so foolishly.

But what all the old timers didn't know was Emperor knew exactly what he was doing and why he was doing it. He and Smoke wanted Juan to feel their presence in the streets, and let him know that he and his sister weren't the only big candy store around.

Emperor knew that eventually both Juan and Ayana were going to start feeling their pockets were getting lighter, and sooner or later, the two of them would be seeking him and Smoke out, trying to figure out who they were, and that's exactly what he wanted.

But what he was so apparently oblivious to was the fact that he was already being tracked by someone in a black Jaguar XF with tinted windows, the driver carefully studying him, just waiting for the opportunity to make a move.

On a warm misty afternoon in the city, rain sprinkled from gray clouds as a hard-face, dark skinned guy in a new Sean Jean jacket twirled a colorful Polo umbrella on the corner.

Behind him, down the block working at customary intervals, more menacing faces in Gucci and North Face jackets stood in the threshold and on the porches of vacant houses and run-down brick buildings.

After all, even a little rain couldn't put a damper on Parkgrove and Gratiot Avenue's open-air drug market.

Emperor's pearl Ferrari 599, sitting on white and gold deep-dish Asanti rims, was parallel parked in the middle of the block, with Triple C's "Can't Trust A Soul" blaring out the windows from the set of 12-inch subwoofers pounding in the trunk.

Two of their soldiers sped up the block doing tricks on high-performance motorcycles, as he and Smoke stood on the sidewalk amidst the live activity in front of an old burgundy ranch-style home, watching as their main trap house up the block do extraordinary numbers, selling bundles of heroin.

It was like watching the welfare line on the first of the month, bevies of dope fiends paraded around the trap house waiting to he served. That house alone made Emperor and Smoke each over $25,000 a day on the regular basis, and they had ten more just like it that was doing almost the same numbers.

Business wise, things couldn't have been better, but psychologically, Emperor was grieving on the inside for Sintana. He missed her so much. There wasn't a day that went past that he didn't think about her, never a second she wasn't on his mind. She was always there, like a shadow following him everywhere he went.

"You all right, bro?" Smoke asked him. He had gotten used to Emperor fading in and out sometimes, daydreaming about Sintana. It happened on the regular.

"N'all man. I'm ready to get to the bottom of this shit. My sister's been dead for what, almost three months now? And we still don't know who killed her." He said frustrated. "And where in the hell is this nigga Juan? How in the fuck this nigga controlling the city, and he ain't never around? What type of muthafucka is that?"

"Like you told me before, we just have to be patient, Emperor, and everything is going to fall in place. We've already done all we could do to get their attention, we can't do nothing now, but wait."

For a second, Emperor became quiet. Something in his aura changed. Smoke knew he was planning something. "What? Why you looking like that?"

"I know something we ain't done yet..." he hinted.

Smoke was confused. "What's that?"

"Juan bought Sintana a beauty salon for her birthday a few months ago... I been checking it out for the past couple days..."

"All right?" Smoke responded, not seeing where he was going. "So what?"

"So, I went through Sintana's stuff that I kept when we cleared out her apartment, and I found the deed to the building and her ownership papers to the business. Legally, we can go in there and take it over. I talked to a lawyer about it this morning."

"Who's running the salon right now?"

"I don't know, but it's been open everyday. All I ever see is women going in and out of it."

"So when are you thinking about taking it over, and how do you plan on doing it?"

Emperor smiled, folding his arms. "I say we just walk up in there right now with the paperwork and make all them muthafucka's get out. Once they see what I have, they won't have a choice but to call Juan, or Ayana, bringing them straight to us."

"I don't know Emperor, man, this could turn out bad. I think we should just wait." Smoke suggested.

"Fuck waiting! I'm tired of waiting. We just goin' go over there and clear that muthafucka out... Let them muthafuckas know we mean business, and if Juan or Ayana got something to say about it, they can come straight to us."

After listening to him, Smoke gave in. He knew it wasn't any negotiating with Emperor once he had his mind made up. "Okay man. You know I'm with you no matter what."

*****

Trying to maintain her composure amid the swirl of children and loud bustle in the bright, central-aired salon, Carmena sipped a glass of Brunello Di Montalcino while standing in the middle of the floor conversing with one of her regular clients, a wealthy Persian woman with long black hair, sporting a beige two-piece business suit and black heels.

Incredible, she thought, trying to keep her eyes glued on the client, but she couldn't help but to take notice of all the children. Look at them. So many races. The salon had brought in clientele from all sorts of ethnic backgrounds. Brazil had been a marketing genius. The girl was a born businesswoman, Carmena thought.

She sighed at the thought of never seeing her friend again, and felt she it owed to her to keep her memory alive by maintaining the salon's thriving business and carrying it into new worlds, just as Brazil would have wanted.

She watched as Fat Al knelt down and lifted up an eight-year-old boy and playfully judo-flipped him over his shoulder onto the couch next to a young Nigerian girl with two long ponytails waiting to get her hair done.

Brazil would have loved to see this. Many cultures and races all united in one place of harmony. Her salon.

"Fat Al!" One of the kids yelled, laughing. "My turn. Do me, do me!"

As Fat Al picked the boy up, two guys hastily walked through the front door, drawing his attention. He sat the little boy back down and nodded at Carmena. "You know them?"

Carmena turned around to see who he was referring to.

The two highly attractive well-dressed men had stopped at the desk, and were now speaking with the receptionist, who looked up and signaled for Carmena to join them.

She walked over there to see what was going on. "What is it, Malana?" she asked the young black girl who had been there since Brazil opened the place. Brazil had brought Malana over from NIKKI'S HAIR SALON, the place she previously worked at before Juan bought her this one.

"This gentleman right here asked me to see the manager," she said, smiling at one of them.

Carmena extended her hand. "Hi, my name is Carmena Azaria. I am the owner. How may I help you?"

Neither of the two guys bothered to shake her hand. They just stared at her sternly.

"That's funny," one of them said. "If you're the owner, then who am T?"

The question caught her completely off guard. "'Excuse me?"

"My name is Emperor Juarez. The girl who originally owned this salon was my sister. And since she's..." he was going to say "dead" but it hurt too much, so instead he said, "not here anymore. I am the heir of this business."

He held up several documents so that she could see them.

For a second, Carmena was baffled by his verbal ambush. She was stunned he would barge up in there like that, and speak to her as if she had stolen the salon or something. It was heartbreaking, and not to mention, embarrassing. "Look, can we go somewhere and talk privately?" she asked as she suddenly remembered seeing him in the photos on the mantle the night she and Ayana went to her apartment to relay Juan's message. He was in nearly every picture, she vividly recalled.

"There's nothing to discuss. I want everybody out of here, except this young lady right here." He demanded, while pointing at Malana. "She can stay. I like her."

Malana smirked, she liked his style.

Carmena tried another approach. "I knew your sister real well. A lot of us did, and we're just as sad as you are about what happened to her. I was only trying to keep Brazil's memory alive by continuing to run this place... My cousin wanted to shut it down after her death, because we all missed her so much. Put I talked him into letting me take it over. That was the least I could do, considering how tight me and her was. It was never my intention to steal from her, or you for that matter. It's just that we were like family."

"Sintana." Emperor said.

"What?" she said looking at him dumbfounded.

"You keep calling her name Brazil. Her name was Sintana."

"Oh, I'm sorry. It's just that we all knew her as Brazil up until, you know, the incident. No disrespect intended, but what name does it have on that paper you're holding?"

She had him, it was signed "Brazil Sanchez" and not "Sintana Juarez."

FUCK!

"Hmm, thought so."

"I don't know if Sintana would want any of you, meaning you or your family, looking after her business in the wake of her death, considering it's because of your family she's dead... I'm her brother, so from now on, I'm the owner. Understand?" he said firmly.

"Que te pasa, Carmena? Te bien?" Fat Al said, interrupting them.

"Esta bueno. This is Brazil's hermano, Emperor." she informed him, then turned back to Emperor. "I don't know what it is you're thinking about me or my family, but it's obvious you have the wrong idea. We didn't have anything to do with her death, and just like you, we want to know who killed her too. My cousin has been wracking his brain, and doing everything possible to find out who killed her, and why. He loved your sister. We all did...." She let that sink in, then said, "The salon is yours. I have no beef with you. I'm sure she would of wanted you to have it. We'll just get our things and go."

The entire salon had went quiet, even the kids had stopped playing, everybody's attention was focused on their emotional conversation.

Carmena spun around in her stilettos, glancing over the faces of her employees and her bodyguards, and said, "Let's go. Take all your belongings."

All the hair-stylists, barbers, and three manicurists obediently dropped everything, packed their things and walked out without an utter of a word. Carmena was the last one to leave, but before she did, she looked at Emperor and said, "We're not the enemy..." And she fell in behind the crowd.

Emperor turned to Smoke, who just shrugged his shoulders.

"That went better than I thought."

"Sure did." He said, thinking to himself that maybe he was making a terrible mistake. He was starting to get the feeling that Carmena was telling the truth -- Juan didn't know who killed Sintana either.

"Excuse me." The young Nigerian girl who had been waiting to get her hair done said. "Now who's gonna do my hair? My stylist just walked out the door?"

Emperor looked over at Malana standing behind the desk watching him. "You do know how to do hair, right?"

Malana smiled. "Don't worry. I got her."

Chapter Fifteen

Around the perimeter of the backyard-small walled, as in most Michigan neighborhoods, European laurels shivered miserably in the brisk wind.

Near the southwest corner, the short pair of azaleas lashed the air, shedding oblong leaves as forest-green as the back of an iguana. In shadows cast by the trees, and behind several of the larger scrubsm were places in which someone could easily hide.

The previously custom-built, 5,000-square-foot luxury home sat on a full acre in the flourishing community of Bloomfield Hills on a residential street composed with many other exquisite estates.

Naturally adapted to dry conditions and accustomed to only water that was provided by the sprinkler system, choirs of toads chanted from hidden niches, scores of shrill vocals that were usually pleasant but seemed spooky and ominous now. Amidst the aria rose the wail of distant sirens echoing beyond.

If the intruder needed to get away before the police got there, the possible routes of escape were limited. The house was protected by a number of guards who were mostly stationed at the Front gate in a post, but others were scattered about throughout the grounds.

Early downpours had lured snails from moist and scarce retreats where they usually remained until, well after nightfall.

Their pale, jellied bodies were stretched most of the way out of their shells, thick feelers questing ahead.

Unavoidably, the shadowy armed figure stepped on a couple, smashing them to slimy pulps, the intruder's mind flashed superstitious notions of godlike entities appearing from the sky at anytime and crushing them with equal indifference.

When the figure came around the corner at the side of the house flanked by a four-car garage, they expected to run into one of the guards, but it was deserted. The patio door was half open.

Once inside, the armed figure pressed the button on the communicator, and whispered into the mic. "Okay, I'm in..."

*****

Down the block a white cargo van that was parked behind some trees came alive. behind the wheel, the driver anxiously stepped on the accelerator, and the van took off with tremendous speed, burning rubber so loud birds scoured from secret places into the air, batting their wings with intensified stokes as they flapped away over the land. The driver swung the vehicle with a hard left turn and crashed into the guard post, creating a perfect diversion.

*****

Hidden in the kitchen pantry, the intruder heard the loud commotion outside and patiently watched as all the guards took off running out the patio door and in other directions to see what was going on. The figure smiled under the mask, people were so predictable.

Now alone, the armed figure slipped out the pantry, careful to close the door back, before creeping along the narrow hall. A television could be heard somewhere close, the figure gripped the handle of the 9mm tightly and crouched lower to the floor as a room on the right side was just ahead. It was a theater-room. The movie, "Miami Vice," was playing on the huge projector mounted on the wall, the final minutes of the cinema. In the dark, the screen flashed bright action scenes and theme music exploded, making the intruder feel somewhat uneasy. Someone was sitting on the couch directly in front of them with their attention diverted on what was happening in the movie.

The armed figure quietly and meticulously moved in closer, carefully easing to the rear of the couch with the gun drawn at the back of the person's body as they leaned forward with their eyes glued to the screen, focused on the action-packed conclusion of the movie.

A smile crossed her lips when she identified her target, and with anticipation, she pressed the gun to his head, awaking him to her presence. "Don't move, and you better not say anything!"

The cold steel sent off alarming signals to his senses, but he maintained his composure as if this deadly encounter was somewhat expected. He wasn't afraid.

Since she hadn't pulled the trigger, he figured there must be something she wanted, so he said, "Who are you, and what is it that you want from me?"

"I told you I was gonna' find you, didn't I?"

Emperor couldn't believe who the voice belonged to. "Ayana?"

"Huh, you think you can just take my money and get away with it? That they'll be no consequences? Who'd you think you were dealing with? If it wasn't for the love my brother had for your sister, I would of killed you. I been following you for days no, and by the way, you need to tighten up on security around this place, I found it relatively easy to get to you."

This girl's got nuts, he thought, laughing. And she was right. There was no way she was supposed to get to him as easy as she did. If I make it through this, I'm firing all these niggas! "Well, you haven't killed me, so what can I do for you?" he thought he'd ask since she still had the gun pressed to the back of his head.

"Haven't killed you yet, you mean… Where's my money?"

He couldn't help but to smile. She was something else. "I have it, but why don't you sit down and have a drink with me?" he offered.

Is this muthafucka crazy! she thought. He takes my money and now he wants to drink with me? What in the hell's wrong with him? "No drinks, just get my money!" she demanded.

"Only if you sit down and have a drink with me," he said seriously. "Or you can kill me, your choice."

She hadn't counted on this, he was persistent, and didn't seem to care she was holding a gun to the back of his head. Usually guys would be shitting their pants by now, begging for their lives. This was unusual, kind of awkward, but she had to admit, she was digging his style. "One drink," she said, "then I want my money."

Emperor hit the button on the remote and all the lights came on. He turned the movie off and got up to get them drinks. Ayana kept the gun trained on him to be sure he wouldn't try anything.

"You know, when my sister got killed, I was thinking all sorts of things..." he said, pouring two glasses of White Russian vodka. "But now... I don't know what to think. At first, all roads led to you and your brother... for obvious reasons..."

"Me and my brother had nothing to do with Brazil's death, so don't ..."

"Let me finish," he said, cutting her off.

Something else she wasn't accustomed to. No one ever cuts her off.

He walked over and handed her drink to her. "I didn't know how to get in touch with either of you directly, so I started targeting your drug establishments, in hopes that someone would lead me to either of you... The night we robbed you, I had no way of knowing who you were. We didn't find out until later that you were who we were looking for. But the robbery was already committed, so I had no choice but to stick with the decision I had made."

"What the fuck is that, your way of apologizing or something?"

"No, I'm not apologizing, because I feel what I did was absolutely necessary, considering the circumstances, and my lack of knowledge. But what I'm saying is, had I known how to find you or Juan, I wouldn't had to resort to those types of measures. But since I didn't, I did what I had to do," he explained. "I don't have to tell you that this is personal for me. That was my sister, and if you were in the same predicament as me, you would of done the same thing, or something much worse, judging by what I heard about you."

Despite everything she felt at the moment, she knew he was right. She would have done anything to find the person responsible if something were to happen to Juan. She sympathized with him on that, but the fact still remained, he had robbed her and Carmena at gun point, then took off in her car. How was she supposed to look past that? How was she supposed to forgive that?

Emperor allowed her a moment to think. He stood in front of her, twirling his glass of White Russian, watching her, her slanting eyes, as dark as they were, were beautiful. She reminded him of the sumptuous Colombian video vixen, Katherine Monsalve, who posed in SMOOTH magazine, except Ayana's hair was black and shiny.

"One million dollars…" she said, after a few seconds of contemplation.

"What?" he frowned, not knowing what she was implying.

"You took three hundred and ninety-thousand from me at Coney Island and your soldiers have robbed many of my drug establishments, so for my inconvenience, and your lack of judgement and knowledge, I'm going to need one million dollars altogether to make us square. I hope that's not a problem," she reasoned, the gun still trained on him, pointed at his chest now.

He nodded. "No, that's understandable. I'll …"

"DON'T MOVE, BITCH! PUT THE GUN DOWN!" Smoke said, bursting into the room.

Ayana laughed and quickly moved to Emperor's side, the gun aimed at his head again. "See what you made me do?" she said. "I seem to have gotten lost in our discussion, and dropped my guard. Let that be a lesson." Emperor gave Smoke a reassuring look. "It's all right. We were just talking. This is Ayana, Juan's sister."

Once Smoke was satisfied everything was cool, he lowered his weapon, holding it at his side. "What the fuck, bro?"

At that same moment, several guards rushed in with a struggling Carmena, who they had restrained, firmly gripping both of her arms. "She must be with her?" one of them said.

"It's cool. Let her go." Emperor ordered.

"Ayana, you all right?" Carmena asked warily.

"I will be, just as soon as they give me my money hack..." she looked at Emperor. "Plus the interest we discussed."

He and Smoke had long been sitting on a small fortune since the day they took the $390,000 from her, so it wasn't going to be nothing to pay her back. He turned to Smoke, who was pissed he had missed the whole conversation, and said, "Get this lady one million dollars for her trouble."

Smoke looked at him like he was crazy. "What!"

"You heard what I said, bag up one million dollars and give it to her."

He wanted to tell Emperor he was trippin', but he sucked it up and did as he was asked, seeing as though they were probably starting to get somewhere in the mystery surrounding Sintana's death.

"It's only going to take him a minute."

"Good," Ayana said. She put her gun away, took a seat on the couch, and downed the rest of her vodka. Carmena walked around to the other sofa, sat down on it, and exhaled from the chain of exciting events. She crossed her legs and rubbed a hand over her knee.

That was when Emperor spotted it. He couldn't believe he hadn't seen it before. The blood in his body began to boil, his eyes instantly going red. He couldn't contain himself, he stormed over and grabbed her hand quick and hard, then pulled a Glock-21 from his waistband. "How in the fuck you get my sister's ring?"

The question and his aggressive motion caught her completely by surprise. "Let me go!"

"Wait!" Ayana said, trying to see what he was talking about. She was shocked to see that he had been armed the entire time. "What ring?"

He held her hand in the air. "This one. My mother gave this to Sintana the day she graduated from the police academy. It's one of a kind. How in the hell did she get it?"

Ayana took a good look at it, and sure enough, she recalled that Brazil use to wear the sentimental piece of jewelry all the time. She wondered why she hadn't noticed it before. "How did you get that, Carmena?"

"Ghost." she said sadly. "Ghost gave it to me a couple months ago. It was a gift. I didn't know it belonged to Brazil." She removed the ring from her finger and gave it to him. "I'm sorry," she said teary-eyed.

"Ghost? Where did Ghost get it from?" Ayana asked her.

"What's going on?" Smoke said, returning with the money. "Here." He handed the garbage bag to Ayana.

Emperor started to calm himself, realizing he had lost control. He released her hand. "Brazil's ring. She had it on." he informed him.

"How did Ghost get it, Carmena?"

"I don't know. But I've had it for a while now."

"Who the fuck is Ghost?" Emperor said hostile, letting them know he wanted some answers.

"One of my brother's friends." she said honestly. "He's been with us for some years. I don't know how he got it."

"That nigga either killed my sister, or he had something to do with it. Where is he now?"

"On the yacht with Juan. They suppose to go to Las Vegas tomorrow. Wait, I'll call him." Carmena said.

"No! I want to gee this nigga's face when we confront him, and ain't no telling what he'll do if you let him know that we're on to him, and I'm not willing to take that chance. He might he the only thing standing between me and what really happened to Sintana."

"He's right, Carmena. We can't do this over the phone." Ayana grabbed Emperor's hand. "Come on, I'll take you to him."

"Good. We'll take my car."

Ayana tossed the keys to the Jaguar Yl7 to Carmena. "You two meet us there." She and Emperor raced out the room to the four car garage where he and Smoke kept their small assortment of luxury vehicles. His pearl Ferrari 599 was the second car after Smoke's ice-blue Aston Martin Vanquish. He hit the "START" button on his

key ring and the sports car fired up like a fighter-jet, then he popped the locks on both doors, and quickly got in. He threw the car in gear, stepping on the peddle, shooting straight out the garage past all his soldiers, through the gate and guard post where Carmena had crashed the cargo van.

It was nightfall when they arrived. It would have been pitch black outside, except the blacktop parking lot had a seam of lights illuminating the area.

The yacht, of which, had the name, "LA BELLE DE BRAZIL," painted at the far corner, near the bottom in script lettering was docked along a pier on Lake St. Clair. The vessel was gigantic. Not an ordinary boat. That had to be worth at least twenty million, Emperor Figured. All white with nautical shades on the side. Ayana led the way. Emperor followed behind her with his anticipation running high.

As they stepped on board, he spotted two of Juan's bodyguards; one on the top level of the boat; the other, near the door, of which he and Ayana were on there way to. "Where's Juan?" she asked the man dressed in a black suit.

"Sitting at the bar with Ghost."

She and Emperor stepped inside, he could see two guys lounging on stools having drinks. One of the guys had on an all-white suit with no tie, the top button of his shirt open, a gold rosary hung from his neck. He and Ayana resembled each other very much, Emperor assumed him to be Juan. The other guy, who looked to be medium height, with a dark-hued face, and athletic physique was casually dressed in a tan pair of khakis and cream shirt. He had to be Ghost, he thought as he sized the two up.

"Ayana, what's wrong?" The guy in white stood up asking her, noticing the anxiety on her face.

She ignored her brother's question and decided to confront Ghost who was checking Emperor out. "Show him the ring." she said.

Emperor held it up so Ghost could see it.

"How did you get this?" She asked him straightforward.

Juan said, "Ayana what's going on? Who is he?"

This time she decided to answer him. "This is Emperor, your now deceased fiancé's brother."

Juan gave Emperor a confused stare.

Ghost just sat there finishing his drink as if he hadn't heard her.

"Where did you get this, Ghost?" she asked him again, this time with more assertiveness in her voice.

He looked her directly in the eye, Emperor too, and said, "I don't know what you're talking about."

"Carmena ain't goin' lie. 'She said you gave it to her.''

Ghost chuckled. "I ain't give that bitch shit. She's lying."

"Bitch? Oh, now my cousin's a bitch?" Ayana said scalding. "No, you the bitch, nigga!"

"Like I said, that bitch is lying!"

"Ghost, watch it, man!" Juan said, surprised by what he was hearing. This wasn't the ghost he has known. It was like another person had entered his body and was speaking for him.

"Look, man, we just want to know how you got it," Emperor tried to reason with him. "It was my sister's."

A strange smile surfaced on Ghost's lip. "Umm-umm-umm..." he said. "Damn, I miss Brazil, don't you, Juan?"

At that, Juan lost it as he started to realize what Ghost had done. "Bitch ass nigga, you killed her!" he reached his hands out in an attempt to choke him, but Ghost was quick on his feet. He swiftly pulled a chrome .45 Desert Eagle from behind him and fired two quick shots, one bullet hit a lamp that was on a table next to one of the sofas, shattering it into pieces, the other one caught Juan high in his left shoulder." AHHHSHIT!" he yelled from the impact and burning sensation.

Ghost took off toward the back room, slamming the door behind him. Smoke, Carmena, and the two guards from outside ran into the room with their guns drawn. Ayana kneeled down at Juan's side, making sure he was all right.

"You stay with him." Emperor told her. "Come on Smoke."

He took his weapon out his Jacket and he and Smoke crossed sides as they made their way to the room door that Ghost dashed into.

As they approached, two more shots rang out inside the room, one slammed through the wooden door, the other sounded like it exploded through a window. Emperor recoiled his leg back, then he kicked the door as hard as he could, forcing it open. He and Smoke ran in ready for a gunfight. The room was empty, and a faint sound of water splashing came from outside the shattered-glass window. He and Smoke ran back the way they had come, past Ayana, Juan, Carmena, and the security, out the door, their eyes searched the river for Ghost, but didn't see him anywhere. He was gone.

They went back inside, Juan was barely standing, looking like he was starting to go in and out of consciousness. Ayana said, "We have to get him to the hospital, he's bleeding everywhere." Emperor helped her get him to the back seat of the Ferrari, then they hurried and got in. Carmena and Smoke hopped in the Jaguar, while the two bodyguards lumped in their black on black Suburban. Both vehicles pulled off right behind the Ferrari.

Once the coast was clear and they had all left, Ghost climbed out the river, laughing to himself about the whole incident. He had been waiting for this day for a long time. He jogged over to his cherry Range Rover, got in, started it, and stepped on the gas. This was far from over. He knew they were heading for the nearest hospital. All he had to do was follow them to see which one.

Andolian Napraja

Chapter Sixteen

Juan couldn't believe that Ghost had the audacity to pull something like that. As he lay in the hospital bed at St. Mary's General with his shoulder taped in gauze, all sorts of questions and scenarios began surfacing in his head. Why would he kill Brazil? She was innocent...

He couldn't help but to think that Ghost had set up the Rasco robbery years ago so he could get close to him.

But none of it made any sense. Why would that nigga go through all of this? It got to be something much bigger going on here...

All these things and more were running through his mind as Ayana, Carmena, Emperor, and the rest of the gang entered the room, interrupting him from his thoughts. Ayana looked worse than he did. Her complexion seemed to be a lot darker than usual, her face tight, and she had the glare of death in her eyes. "Ghost had the nerve!" She thought. "I'm going to find him and kill him and his whole fuckin' Family... That ought to teach the next stupid son of a hitch about fuckin' with mine!"

Like her brother, she had a lot of questions concerning Ghost as well, but right now she just wanted to make sure Juan was okay. He and Carmena was all she had left in the world. Neither of them had any other living relatives that they knew about. She and Juan's parents had been shot to death years ago in their home, and

Carmena's mother was killed when she was younger. Since then, it had been just the three of them.

It broke her heart to see her brother lying up in a hospital bed. When they were kids she vowed to always protect him, even if it meant sacrificing her own life.

Despite his current predicament, Juan still managed to find humor in the situation. "That bitch ass nigga tricked the shit out of us, didn't he, sis?" he said with a half-cocked smile.

But Ayana wasn't in the mood for jokes, she wanted vengeance for Ghost's sinister act or treason. "We're gonna get him, Juan, don't worry. He's a dead man walkin'... I promise," she swore.

A nurse came in to check his gauze. She was a short white girl with mixed-blond and brunette-colored hair that was cut evenly around the edges and hanging over her shoulders. "Hello, I'm Nurse Cindy. How are you feeling, Mr. Azaria?" she asked pleasantly.

"I'm all right."

"Any dizziness or pain?"

"N'all, I feel good. How long do I have to stay here?"

"Probably until tomorrow sometime. We have to run a few more tests." She plopped his pillow and adjusted his blankets for him. "You should get some sleep. I have to warn you, in the next couple hours, a few police officers will be here to ask you some questions."

That raise his eyebrows. "Why? What's up?"

"Don't worry, it's standard. We have to put the police department on notice anytime we receive a gunshot victim. They like to get here quickly before the victim can leave."

"That's fine." Ayana said. "Do you mind if I have a moment alone with my brother, please?"

Nurse Cindy gave her a warm smile. "Certainly." she said, then looked at the rest of the gang. "But all of you are going to have to leave. I'm sorry, visiting hours are over. He needs rest. You all can see him in the morning."

Emperor and Smoke nodded at him as they walked out.

Carmena went over and hugged him, then she left, along with the two bodyguards. "We'll be out here if you need us, boss."

Juan nodded his head at him.

"Okay. I'll be back in a few minutes." Nurse Cindy informed them.

Ayana stood next to him holding his hand. "I'm going to have to leave you here for a few hours. I'm taking a team over to his house. I doubt if he'd be stupid enough to be sitting there, but still, I have to check all angles. But in the meantime, I'm gonna call Fat Al, and tell him to get down here immediately with a few guys and provide you with adequate security. You'll be safe. If you need me, -just have one or them to call. I'm going to leave the two guards here with Carmena until Fat Al and the others arrive. Then they're going to escort her home."

"I'll be all right, sis. Go take care of whatever you have to. Find that hoe ass nigga. But if you can, keep him alive for me. I want to deal with him myself. This is personal."

"I'll try," she grinned. "Here. You're going to need this, just in case." Ayana slid a .45 auto under his sheets.

Juan took it and held it tightly in his hand. He loved his sister. She was always thinking ahead.

Nurse Cindy returned. "I'm sorry, but you have to go now," she said to Ayana.

"I was just leaving." Ayana gave him a hug. "See you in the morning."

Outside the room, Ayana called Fat Al and told him where they were and what happened. "I need you here at the hospital with Juan while I make a few runs."

"No problem," he said. "I'll bring three guys with me."

"Good. And also bring a security detail so the nurses won't give you any problems."

"You got it."

She hung up the phone and turned her attention to the two bodyguards. "You two stay here and stand guard. Fat Al will be here in a minute with a few other guys. Then I want you two to take Carmena home and stay with her, comprende?"

"Si, señora," one of them said. "No problemo."

"Anything we can do?" Emperor asked.

"Yeah. I need you both to come with me. We're going to check Ghost's house out. See if we can get lucky."

Carmen walked up. "What about me, Ayana? What do you want me to do?"

"I want you to stay here until Fat Al and the others show up. Make sure they don't have any problems with the nurses. They're bringing a legal-binding security detail to protect Juan. They're all licensed to carry firearms, so there shouldn't be any problems. Once they get here and everything is fine, call me and let me know. Then I want you to go home and wait. Take those two with you. It'll be enough security here to look out for Juan. I doubt if anything will happen, but it's best to be prepared."

She turned to Emperor and Smoke, who seemed highly impressed by the way she handled business. "Come on, you two. We have somewhere to be."

Ghost lived in a two-story center-entrance Colonial home out in Cross Point Farms. Ayana, Emperor, Smoke, and her team of eight female soldiers pulled up in four separate vehicles outside the residence simultaneously. They all got out and surrounded the premises. Four girls crept along the rear, while the other four stayed with Ayana, Emperor, and Smoke out front.

"I want you two to stay out here, just in case he's in there, and he tries to escape."

"Si, señora," one of them said.

She turned to the other two. "All right, knock the door down," she instructed.

The two girls ran in front of them with their guns drawn. They stopped at the door, one standing on each side. The taller one of the two nodded at the other as she stepped in front of the door and blew the lock away with a double-barrel shotgun. BOOM! BOOM! The other chick then kicked it open.

Ayana, Emperor, and Smoke followed them inside.

At the same time, two of the four female soldiers in the back did the exact same thing to the rear door, while the remaining two stayed outside to keep watch.

It was dark inside, Ayana hit the light switch in the foyer. With a gun in her hand, she listened for movement of any kind. She heard nothing. "Search every room in this place!" she ordered them. "If he's here, I want him!"

Emperor and Smoke headed upstairs to take a look around. They each searched both of the two bedrooms, checking the closets, under the beds, and behind the curtains. They found nothing. He wasn't there. In fact, it looked like no one had been there in a while. There wasn't any kind of mail lying around or any kind of paperwork that you'' usually find in someone's home. Ghost had thought of everything, Emperor thought. He was most likely living somewhere else. They went back downstairs to join Ayana who was in the contemporary-style kitchen, checking the refrigerator. There wasn't anything in it.

"He hasn't been here in a long time." Emperor stated the obvious.

"Yeah, this is a dead-end," Smoke said.

Ayana picked up a glass angrily and threw it against the wall, shattering it. "That son of a bitch!" she screamed pissed. She wanted to find him and cut him into little pieces, then feed his flesh and bones to rats. That would ease her anxiety.

But what she and the rest of them didn't know, was Ghost was parked outside, down the block, watching them. He had been in the hospital with them the whole time, watching from afar.

Smiling to himself, he felt good knowing he had covered all his tracks. There was no way they'd be able to find him.

Satisfied, he eased the Range Rover away with the headlights off and turned down a side street, disappearing in the night as if he was never there.

Chapter Seventeen

"YOU DID WHAT? WHAT WERE YOU THINKING RICARDO - GIVING THAT GIRL THAT FUCKIN' RING! ARE YOU STUPID, OR JUST MAD?" Cholo hissed, slamming his fast hard on the kitchen table, glaring at Ghost after he told him what he had done.

"I promise you papi, they don't know you had anything to do with her death. They ain't got a clue you're my father."

"That was stupid, Ricardo. You shouldn't have done that. Now they're going to wonder why you did all of this. Your reason for killing that girl. Sooner or later, he's going to find out you're my son, and then everything we built will be at stake." Cholo just couldn't understand why Ghost would pull something like that. He and Claudia had worked hard to build their empire. Ghost was playing with fire. Once Ayana got to digging around, and Cholo knew she would, she was going to unveil the truth behind who killed their parents. That was something Cholo couldn't let happen. "You have to fix this, Ricardo. And you have to do it fast."

"Don't worry, papi. And I have everything under control. By tomorrow, you're going to be thanking me."

His father looked at him warily. He knew that it was too late to turn back now. It was all or nothing.

"All I ask is one thing…" Ghost said.

Cholo sighed, disappointed in him. "What?"

"When this is all over, and Juan and Ayana are dead, I ask that you turn their share of the real estate company over to me."

Cholo nodded. "If you clean all this up, without a scratch of my name being mentioned in the process, you have my word. Their share of the company is all yours."

Ghost smiled. "That's all I needed to know." He turned and walked away.

Cholo sat there thinking for a minute. God, he hoped his son didn't fuck everything up. "Julio!" he shouted for his middle-aged servant.

"Yes, Mr. Dominguez?" Julio appeared in the doorway.

"Get Claudia on the phone. Tell her we have a problem."

*****

For a second, Ghost stood in the middle of the floor in his bedroom at his parents' house, premeditating what he was going to do next. Then he slid open the mirror closet door, and behind his clothes that were on hangers, there was a large wall-safe. He dialed the five-digit combination and opened it. Inside was $50,000 in cash, a Colombian passport, and several weapons, including three flash grenades. Ghost grabbed two 9mm Berettas, a Mack-11 with an extended clip, and one flash grenade. He made sure that weapons were all loaded, then tucked the two Berettas in his waistband and hung the Mack-11 over his shoulder by its strap.

In the back of the closet, he had two Kevlar bulletproof vests. He snatched one of them off the hanger and left the other. He put it on, then put his black coat over everything and placed the flash grenade in the pocket.

Checking the time on his G-Shock, it read 9:36 a.m. Perfect. After he went out and stole a car, he could still make it to the hospital before three.

*****

Two uniformed police officers entered Juan's room. Both were young white dudes. One had short, dark-blond hair with a clean-shaved face. The other cop's hair was longer and black, but tapered on the sides. He wore a pair of wire-framed glasses and had a shaggy-lined goatee.

Juan was still awake. Nurse Cindy had warned him earlier that he would be receiving a visit from them, so he stayed up - going over everything in his mind that he planned to tell them.

The black-haired cop said, "How are you, Mr. Azaria? I'm Officer Gentz, and this is my partner, Officer Reeves. You want to tell us how you got shot?"

"Some guy broke into my yacht. Apparently, he didn't know that me and my sister was on board. When I came out to confront him, the guy started shooting. I caught one in the shoulder."

"I see," he said.

Officer Reeves stood off to the side and just jotted everything down in his miniature notepad.

Gentz continued, "So you were on your yacht... And what time was this, approximately?"

"Uh, it was about... nine-thirty, I think. It had just turned night outside."

Again, Reeves wrote it down, looking up at him every so often, reading him.

Officer Gentz sort of smirked, figuring he'd ask the obvious. "And how is it you can afford a yacht? You look a little young..."

Now Juan was smiling. "I am young. Shit, I'm not even thirty yet. But I happened to be the co-owner of Millennium Real Estate International... You heard of us, right? Oh, and I'm also the number one shareholder of Galaxy Sports Promotional Incorporation in Last Vegas. Check me out if you want to," he said boastfully. Juan loved stuntin' on cops. It wasn't nothing like seeing the stupid looks on their faces when he crushed them.

"Oh... I'm sorry... Mr. Azaria... but I had to... had to... ask... I didn't mean any... any disrespect. It's just ... unusual that someone... someone... your age... would own... would own a yacht."

"Did you see what the guy looked like? Was he black, Hispanic?" Officer Reeves said, figuring his partner needed some assistance since he seemed to have gotten caught up in a web of cluttered words.

"White. He was definite white," Juan said, almost laughing. He found it funny that Officer Reeves thought only a black or Hispanic guy could be the culprit, and not a white dude. It was purely racial profiling. "Yeah, he was white. A dirty ass white boy, too," he rubbed it in.

Both of the officers gave each other a skeptical look. They couldn't believe he was going to blame this one a white kid.

"Really, Mr. Azaria? Are you sure he was white?"

"Oh, I'm definitely sure. He had the stupidest face I ever seen. And only a white kid would stink the way he did."

They looked at him with their mouths wide open, stunned.

*****

Ghost parked the stolen Jeep Grand Cherokee just outside the emergency entrance on the side of a Monte Carlo. He sighed, and thought for a second maybe he shouldn't go through with this. But he had to. Everything that he had done his whole life led up to this moment.

With that in mind, he casually walked through the double-sliding electric doors.

Triage was busy, doctors and nurses were scattered about in all directions holding charts and overseeing patients. Gurneys with sick people sat out in the hall as he strolled past making his way to the nearest elevator. Juan's room was on the third floor. When the elevator doors open, two doctors stepped out, talking among each other, never noticing him. He quickly walked in and pressed number 3 on the panel.

As he waited for the doors to re-open his adrenaline pumped rigorously anticipating his actions.

Ding! The doors opened. He stepped out and walked up the hall, cautious not to accidentally run into any of Juan's bodyguards prematurely. They would easily recognize him and it could throw his plans off. That was something he didn't need.

Strolling past the packed waiting-room, he met eyes with a young boy sitting on his mother's lap. Ghost smiled at the kid and kept going to the end of the hall where there was another hall intersecting it. Juan's room was just to the left, right across from the nurse's station.

Ghost swiftly darted into a maintenance room and readied his weapons. He cocked the two Berettas and tucked them back in his waist, then positioned the Mack-11 around his shoulder so he could easily grab it when it was time.

As he stepped out the maintenance room, two police officers were leaving Juan's room.

They walked past the four bodyguards who were all posted by the door, talking.

Once the police were out of sight, Ghost came around the corner with a flash-grenade in his hand. He pulled the pin and rolled it across the floor.

It hit the foot of one of the guards and as he looked down to see what it was, it exploded, BOOM!

Instantly the fire alarms went off, echoing loudly through the building. Sprinklers squirted heavy splashes of water immersing the floors. The guards were in a frenzy, speaking in Spanish, trying to see through the smog, their guns drawn and ready.

Ghost spat the Mack-11, BLAT-TAT-TAT! BLAT-TAT-TAT! Catching one of them high in the chest, knocking him to the puddled floor. BLAT-TAT-TAT-TAT! Another burst of gunfire erupted, hitting another one.

They died never seeing him.

"WHERE IN THE HELL ARE YOU?" The last one standing yelled as he returned a round of gunfire into the haze of smoke. BOOM! BOOM! BOOM!

Doctors and nurses ran from every direction, coughing and choking. Patients screamed, panicking for their lives.

As the fog of smoke finally started to subdue, the bodyguard caught sight of his assailant. He couldn't believe it was only him by himself. He expected to see a small army. "YOU SON OF A BITCH!" He charged toward Ghos, firing rapidly. BOOM! BOOM! BOOM!

Ghost quickly got out the way.

The guard kept firing. BOOM! BOOM! CLICK! CLICK!

FUCK!

The gun was empty.

Ghost laughed as he ran up and emptied the Mack-11 in the guy's face.

He slid down the wall and fell sideways, dropping the empty weapon.

Where's Fat Al? He must have run into Juan's room, he figured. He grabbed the door handle. It was locked, or Fat Al was holding it on the other side. Either way, Ghost blew the lock away with one of the Berettas. BOOM! BOOM! He kicked it open.

Fat Al was standing in the middle of the room, holding a .45 auto. He let off two shots. BOOM! BOOM! "DIE, MUTHAFUCKA, DIE!"

Ghost stepped to the side of the doorway, dodging both bullets.

"FREEZE! PUT THE GUN ON THE GROUND!" Suddenly, the two cops he had seen earlier appeared from nowhere.

He dashed into Juan's room, shooting wildly at Fat Al. BOOM! BOOM! BOOM!

Fat Al grabbed Juan out of the bed and stood in front of him, shielding him. "You're gonna have to kill me first!" he yelled at Ghost, who was ducking behind a small wooden desk in the corner of the room.

"Then so be it, nigga," he squeezed off three quick rounds, hitting Fat Al in the stomach and in the face. He fell to the ground, his eyes wide open, staring at Juan's bare feet.

Juan stood there calm. He refused to show any signs of weakness. "Before you kill me, just tell me one thing. Why? Why are you doing all this?"

Ghost stood up, looking at him. "Cholo Dominguez is my father. Figure it out, nigga!"

"What?" he said, confused.

"You're so stupid… Who do you think killed your parents? Do you think me and you met by accident… My father's been planning this since you and I were kids… He sent Claudia to kill your mother and father… Took their company, then taught you how to run it… Don't you see, you been my father's bitch your whole life!"

BOOM! BOOM! BOOM!

The 9mm under Juan's hospital gown erupted, catching Ghost in his mid-section. He fell to the floor, lying on his back. Luckily for Juan, Ayana had left him a little protection.

"FREEZE! DROP THE GUN ON THE GROUND!" one of the two cops barked, just as he was about to unload the rest of his clip into Ghost's motionless body.

He dropped the weapon and put his hands in the air.

"So I guess this is the so-called white perpetrator who shot you in the shoulder, huh?" Officer Reeves said sarcastically. "Looks Hispanic to me. How about you, Gentz?"

"Sure do," Gentz said. "Okay, Mr. Azaria, you can put your hands down. Just have a seat on the bed."

Juan did as he was told, but kept his eyes fixed on Ghost's body. He couldn't believe he was gone. Now all he had to do was get Cholo.

Officer Reeves walked over to remove the gun from Ghost's hand. When he bent over his body, Ghost's eyes suddenly opened, a broad smile appeared on his face as he grabbed Reeves and stuck his Beretta to his chest and squeezed the trigger. BOOM! BOOM! Killing him instantly, scaring the shit out of Officer Gentz. "WHAT THE HELL!"

Ghost rose up from the floor like Michael Myers in what seemed like slow motion.

Terror struck Gentz. He had never seen anything like this in his life. This guy's mad! he thought. Out of fear, he froze, and that cost him his life. Out of nowhere, Claudia Remirez came up behind him and fired a single shot to the back of his head, knocking his uniform hat off.

"Vamos Ricardo! Let's go! Let's go!"

He looked around the room for Juan, but he was gone. The joining room door was open. Damn! He got away.

"Vamos Ricardo! We have to go! SWAT is on their way up!" Claudia yelled.

Shit! Ghost quickly stripped out of his clothes, tossing them on the floor.

"What are you doing? We have to go!" Claudia said.

"I'll never get out of here wearing these... Pass me one of those gowns over there."

Smart, Claudia thought. She passed him a gown, he put it over his naked body, then kicked the clothes and the guns under the bed with the bulletproof vest.

When they got in the hall, he spotted a wheelchair and got in it. Claudia got behind and started pushing him.

A few nurses were still gathering patients from their rooms. One of them came over and helped her with Ghost.

"What's going on?" Claudia asked, playing stupid.

"A madman with a gun just attacked the hospital. We have to get him out of here!" she said frantically, almost shaking.

Just as their turned the corner, SWAT was coming out the stairwell, storming the building, infrared beams on their weapons. The lead officer made eye contact with Ghost and Claudia as they all made their way to the elevator, but kept going.

As they got on the elevator, Ghost looked up and caught a glimpse of Juan and a nurse coming out one of the rooms, still in his hospital gown. For a second, their eyes locked on each other. Hatred to hatred. And then the doors closed, dividing them forever.

Andolian Napraja

Chapter Eighteen

Ayana's ride home with Emperor and Smoke was quiet. Emperor hadn't said much since they left Ghost's empty house. She could tell he was deep in thought as he handled the wheel of the Ferrari with tension. Ayana knew he wanted to resolve this situation with his sister's death more than anything. She could see it in his eyes, and in the way he moved, it was killing him inside.

Though they had just met, she felt a strange connection with him somehow.

Figuring she'd be the one to break the quiet, from the passenger seat, she rubbed her gentle hand over the top of his shoulder tenderly and said, "You okay?" Once the words left her mouth, it suddenly sounded like the wrong thing to ask.

Emperor was so caught in his own thoughts that he didn't think much of it. "I'm straight." he said driftingly.

"We're going to get him. He's not going to get away with this." she assured him.

"Yeah, I know... I just got this feeling that my sister was a pawn in a much bigger game being played here. It feels like he killed her for his own selfish reasons, you know what I mean...."

Ayana sighed, she didn't know what to say, but it was starting to look like he was right.

They pulled up at the gate of her and Juan's mansion. A few guards were outside patrolling the perimeter. One of them peered in the car and saw Ayana's face, then he stepped aside way to let them pull in, Her black Jaguar was parked out front, which meant Carmena had made it back safely.

When they pulled up in front of the house, Ayana opened the car door, and said, "Ya'll should stay here for the night, just in case something comes up. We got a few guest rooms..."

Emperor turned around and looked at Smoke in the back seat. "What do you think? You wanna stay here for the night?"

Smoke nodded. "We can chill." He said, daydreaming about Carmena. He couldn't wait to see her again, she was fine as hell.

Emperor turned to Ayana. "All right. We'll stay."

She was elated to hear that.

They all got out of the car and went in the house. Carmena was stretched out on the couch in the main room, looking as if she had just fallen asleep, and was now interrupted by their sudden intrusion.

Smoke licked his lips at her as their eyes met.

She shot him a warm smile.

Emperor and Ayana noticed their apparent attraction and decided to leave them be. "Come on, Emperor," Ayana said pulling him by the hand. "Let me show you to your room."

Just as they entered the hall, Juan busted through the front door with Nurse Cindy. He was still in his hospital gown. "Y'all ain't goin' believe what just happened!"

Carmena sat up on the couch. Smoke was sitting next to her, and Ayana and Emperor stood in the center or the room.

Juan looked kind of spooked. All he had on besides the gown were a pair of house shoes. Nurse Cindy looked so frightened that she was shaking. Whatever had happened, Ayana thought, must have been something scary. She had never seen that sort of look in her brother's eyes before.

"That nigga Ghost just tried to kill me at the hospital. I mean like came up in there on some terminator shit. This nigga took out all the guards, and a police officer. Then fuckin' Claudia Remirez showed up out of nowhere and killed another one. It was like a movie. I shot that nigga, I don't know how many times. He just laid there on the ground for a second, and then, rose up on some Jason-type of shit, you know... if Nurse Cindy didn't come through the joining door from the other room and got me up out of there... man, I would've been..."

"Calm down, Juan." Ayana said going over to put her arms around him.

"He didn't have no way to get home, so I drove him." Nurse Cindy said, still shaking.

"Thanks, we appreciate everything you've done," Ayana told her.

"It was nothing, really. I was just looking out for my patient," she said with a sly grin, not sure of her own words.

Juan turned to her. "Thank you. My cousin right here is going to give you something for your troubles."

"Oh, that's not necessary."

"No, we look out for those who look out for us," Ayana told her.

Carmena got up from the couch and took her by the hand. They went into one of the back rooms, where there was a safe hidden in a cabinet. Carmena opened it. It was filled with money. She took out several stacks and handed them to her. Nurse Cindy was still trying to process everything. Her eyes were as wide as a deer caught in the headlights. Her mind running in overdrive. "Thank you," she said, tucking the money in her purse.

Carmena gave her a card. "If you ever need us for anything, just call, okay? And I mean anything. We'll be there for you."

Nurse Cindy shook her head. "I won't say anything to the police."

"We know you won't, but we're not worried about that, anyway," Carmena led her back out to the front room with everyone else. Nurse Cindy reached out and gave Juan a big hug. "You be safe now, okay."

"I will. Thank you, again."

She nodded her head at everyone else, then walked out the door.

As soon as she was gone, Juan said, "We have to find that nigga, y'all. This shit is starting to get out of hand now."

"Yeah, but how do we find him?" Emperor asked. "We went to his house, but it was empty. He probably ain't lived there in a long ass time."

"Oh, I knew it was something else I had to tell y'all" Juan shouted abruptly. "Guess what that nigga told me..."

"WHAT!" Everybody said almost in unison.

"That nigga told me Cholo Dominguez is his father. He said that Cholo sent Claudia to murder our parents when we were younger... That he took their company, then showed me how to run it for him. Ain't that some shit!"

Ayana was stuck. She couldn't believe what she was hearing. She had to take a seat on the other couch across from where Smoke and Carmena were, for the first time in her life she felt like a sucker. Cholo had played them like some idiots, and that infuriated her. Everything inside of her wanted them dead. The night their parents were found dead she and Juan had stayed up all night trying to figure out why something so horrible had to happen to them. What did they do to deserve such a dreadful death? "I'm going to kill both of them son of a hitches..." she said, scalding hot.

"Same thing I was thinking." Juan added.

Emperor felt sorry for them. He had no idea that they had been dealing with some of the same issues he was dealing with. At that moment, he felt connected to them. Ayana especially. She had been through so much. He just wanted to hold her and tell her that everything was going to be all right. He took a seat next to her and put his arm around her shoulder, and returned the same words she had given him in the car earlier. "Don't worry, we're going to get them. I swear to you that they're all going to pay."

As much as she wanted to fight it, his words were soothing, and his touch was consoling. She gave into his warm affection, accepting his embrace, and resting her head on the crease of his chest. He stroked his fingers through her hair.

Carmena and Juan looked at each other stunned. Neither of them had ever seen anyone gain Ayana's trust or feelings as fast as Emperor had. I knew there was something different about him, Carmena thought. A person never knew with Ayana, she was so driven. Maybe that was it... Emperor's the same kind of person. Their personalities are just alike, she figured, putting it together.

"Anyway." Juan said, "I think I know how to find them."

"What? How?" Emperor was all ears.

"Cholo loves the opera." He explained. "There's a opera show coming to Detroit in a couple weeks. I'd bet my last dollar that he's going to be there."

"Where's the show going to be?" Smoke chimed in.

"The Detroit Opera House, downtown."

"You're right, Juan. I remember meeting him and Claudia one night at the opera house. He told me himself that he never missed a show." Ayana said.

"When is the show?" Emperor asked.

"On the twenty-fourth. All we have to do is be there. We can kill him right there in the opera house."

Everybody around the room nodded their heads. It sounded like a plan.

All they had to do now was prepare themselves and be ready when the time came, and they would all get the revenge they craved for.

Andolian Napraja

Chapter Nineteen

Claudia gunned the 7-Series BMW, careening through red lights. Her secret hideaway was all the way out in Lakeside. Even without traffic, it was ten minutes away.

She punched Cholo's number in her cell. A busy signal.

She tried again. One of his servants answered and said he had just gone to bed. "Do you want me to wake him, Ms. Remirez?"

"No, listen to me…" she said, swerving, engine purring up the lane through sketchy traffic. "Tell him that I got Ricardo. He was at the hospital… All hell broke loose… He was shot once in the side, but not too hard. He'll be fine… Tell him I'm taking him to the hideaway for a couple days until things cool down. I'll fix him up myself. I don't know if any of the cameras in the hospital picked anything up or not… We may have to get him out of the country. Tell him that, you understand?"

"Si, senora. I'm going to do that this minute. Mr. Dominguez insists on hearing bad news right away."

She clicked the phone off. Her eyes flashed at the clock on the dash. Just a few more minutes and they'll be there. She looked to her side, in her passenger seat, Ghost had his hand pressed against the wound in his mid-section, breathing heavily. "We're almost there. Just hang on," she said.

"I'm good. This shit just stings. I don't know how it got through the vest."

"It's not that bad. It's just a graze. I'm going to fix it up for you. You'll be fine in a couple days, but it's going to leave a nasty scar."

Finally she slowed down a bit and turned onto a dirt road, going past a heap of trees and hills of land. A few minutes later, she made a hard right turn down another road and Ghost could see a large old-style country home.

She pulled the car in beside the house and got out.

Ghost struggled getting his door open. It seemed like every move he made cost him some form of pain.

Claudia helped him in the house.

It was cozy inside. He could see why she liked this place. It had everything, yet it was cut off from the rest of the world. He could be there forever and no one would ever know it. Each room had a different style of furnishing, but they all were elegant in their own way.

She got the fire going in the fireplace to generate a little warmth.

When she was done, she instructed Ghost to have a seat on the dining room table and take off the hospital gown so she could examine his wound thoroughly.

He almost ripped the bloody gown off his body and threw it to the floor. He sat there naked waiting for her.

She turned all the lights on in the room so she could see properly. The bullet had left a long gash by his ribs, dried up blood clotted its crease. She went in the bathroom and grabbed her first aid kit, so she could get a roll of catgut thread and a suturing needle. She found some peroxide and alcohol in the medicine cabinet and a box of gauze.

Ghost leaned his muscular body back and squeezed his stomach tightly as she cleaned the wound. He could feel every piece of the tissue rubbing against his sensitive flesh.

Once the wound was clean, blood started to flow slowly out of it down the side of his stomach. She wiped it away, then asked him to lie back while she began patching him up.

Claudia had done this once before a few years ago, when her boyfriend, Carmelo, came home bleeding badly one night. He had been scratched in the face and had some sort of stab wound on his chest. When Claudia asked him how did it happen, he told her that he got jumped by some guys over in Southwest Detroit in some courtyard at an apartment building. It wasn't until the news came on TV that evening with a 'Breaking Story' that she put everything together for herself. He had killed Mena, his baby's mother. Stabbed her to death like a coward. Claudia was furious. When Carmelo took a bath that night, she busted the bathroom door open and shot him four times in the face with her chrome .380 auto. Carmelo sunk in the tub covered in bloody soap bubbles and water, his eyes staring at her unbelieving.

Killing Carmelo hurt her to the core. She loved him, but she couldn't stand the sight of his face after finding out what he had done to that poor girl. Claudia dumped his body sometime later where the police could find him, and since then she had tried to forget about it.

Now here she was again. Though not in the same house, and the circumstances were different too. But the situation was similar. She pushed and pulled the needle and thread in and out of him, closing him up. The wound swelled up into a puff that looked much like a tiny football with the stitches as the holding part.

When she was done, Ghost got up off the table and walked around the room naked, trying to adapt to the odd feeling. Though he could still feel a slight stinging sensation, it didn't hurt anymore.

Claudia watched him with lustful eyes. His physique was spectacular. He must train and exercise at least five days a week, she thought.

As she watched him, she remembered teaching him how to kill when he was younger. Cholo had insisted on it. Ghost had quickly advanced after only a few months, hitting all his targets and beating all the times and records of others she had trained.

She and Cholo decided to give him a real training exercise using a real life situation. They had recruited a local drug dealer named Rasco, and gave him instructions to rob and kill Juan Azaria. Ghost was told to stop Rasco before he completed the task at all cost. And that he did, blowing the back of Rasco's head off in broad daylight.

Not only had Ghost passed the test of his training, but he gained the undoubting trust of Juan Azaria for saving his life.

Claudia couldn't have been more proud of him, Cholo too. It was that incident that brought the two families together.

Over a year later, Juan and Cholo were partners over at Millennium Real Estate International, the company that Jose Azaria started with his wife. The one they had forcefully seized through blood.

"Damn, you sure know how to fix a nigga up." Ghost said, breaking her from her trance.

"That was something I never got a chance to teach you." She was enjoying him walking through the house with his penis dangling around in plain sight like he didn't have a care in the world. This was something new, she thought. She never looked at him before like she was looking at him now. He wasn't a kid anymore, that's for sure. No, he was a man, and a good looking one too.

Ghost caught her staring out the corners or his eyes. He could feel her eyes roaming all over his body. "I sure can use a hot bath." He said.

"There's a hot tub in the back. Go on back there. I'll get some drinks."

When he left, she went over to the bar and grabbed a bottle of Lerlon Brazilian cachaca and two short glasses.

Ghost was already relaxing with his arms stretched out over the rim of the tub. She kicked off her heels and sat the bottle or cachaca down on the hardwood floor, and then, dropped her dress and thong right in front of him, giving him a tasteful view of her intoxicating body. She was flawless. Beautiful in every way.

When she got in the tub, she turned around and poured them each a glass of Lerlon.

As she took a sip from one, she passed him the other. He took the glass, then pulled her to him. She didn't resist. He was strong and captivating. He stared into her eyes as if he could see through her soul. At last, they kissed, and the world seemed to disappear.

In that moment, only the two of them existed. Nothing else mattered. Ghost caressed her firm ass cheeks, holding them tightly in his hands. Claudia moaned as her stomach rubbed against his already erect dick. As he embraced her, he hungrily sent his tongue spiraling down her throat. She drank his lust and gave in to his desire, allowing him to feed from her mouth. He scooped her up and held her against the wall of the tub, parting her thighs, sliding into her juicy, fat pussy. Her body shivered. It had been a while since she had any dick. She and Ramone hadn't been intimate in months. This was what she needed.

Ghost was putting it down on her, thrusting in and out, plunging her deeply, hitting her in places she hadn't felt in years.

Claudia bounced up and down on his thick-shafted pole like she was saddled on a black Arabian horse.

"Hold up," he sat her on the edge of the tub, then got out.

"What?" she said, wondering what he was doing. She was just getting in her zone. "Why you stop?"

"Chill out, li'l mama, I'm far from done. I just want to get up here, so I can hit yo' ass from the back," he said as he jumped up there with her.

At that, Claudia turned around and positioned herself doggy-style, craving his big dick.

He didn't keep her waiting long, getting behind her, he re-entered her hot, slippery love canal.

She bucked against him, backing that ass up, never getting enough. "Yeah, Ghost... Yeah! Don't stop baby! Yeah! Eww! Oooh ... Yeah!" she screamed pleasurably, her voice bouncing off the walls.

Ghost bit down on his lip and dug into her as much as he could, ramming her buttocks with hard thrusts. He was loving it. He had always wondered if Claudia had some good pussy. Oh, it was definitely good. He wished his niggas could see him now. This was like a dream come true for him - to be fuckin' the legendary Claudia Remirez. Any nigga would love to be in his shoes, or more like his bare feet, right now.

With that in mind, he increased his speed, pounding into her like a mad man. The night was still young.

Chapter Twenty

Two Weeks Later

Ayana stepped out the shower and dried her hair, her mind preoccupied with all the latest events. It had been a crazy two weeks, both emotionally and mentally. First, all the stuff with ghost, that was one thing, then she ended up falling for emperor, which was something totally different. And she was starting to like it.

They had spent the day on a private beach in Puerto Rico. Something had evolved between them. Perhaps it was what he told her about the other chicks he had been with, that he never formed attachments with any of them. Though Ayana changed the subject immediately, not wanting to hear about his exploits with other females, she felt that maybe in some supernatural way that they had been waiting to meet each other. Her only concern was what his plans were with her.

She and Emperor were having fun together, despite everything else that was going on. That was all she could handle at the moment.

Just being in his presence, alone with him, was blissful. She had been besieged by him. Only the two of them together, without interruptions or distractions, not having Carmena, Juan or Smoke around made all the difference.

That hadn't been the case in a long time. This was something foreign to her, for both of them. It was like starting at the beginning, fresh. Everything about him was different. She supposed maybe she was different, too. So many things had happened in both of their lives, they both had been through so much.

A brand new relationship with so many similarities. If that wasn't crazy, what was?

They spent the past couple weeks simply playing and getting to know each other.

During their time spent on the private beach on the sands of San Juan, Puerto Rico, they had gone underwater snorkeling, parasailing, shopping, and toured the entire beautiful island. Ayana probably brought back over three hundred pictures of all the architecture and breathtaking sights and views.

Emperor had been a real gentleman, composed and indulging in everything she wanted to do. She couldn't think of anyone else she wanted to be with. And he truly seemed to enjoy every activity, seemed to love exploring the neighborhoods and cities, seeing all the towns, and taking in the Caribbean atmosphere. They were in sync, especially when it came to shopping, he knew exactly what he wanted. Ayana knew she wasn't dragging him along, that he was having just as much fun as she was. And every second spent with him made her realize how much she needed him in her life.

"Ugh," she said, staring in the mirror, "Try not to think about him..." She had to get ready for their date tonight and she was running late. Emperor was in the other room, and here she was fantasizing in the mirror... what the hell was she fantasizing about anyway? Everything and nothing as usual, lately. Overthinking everything, of course, as she always did. She drove herself crazy.

She dried her hair, then pulled the sides of it back into a nice, tight ponytail. Pretty, but not too much. She stared at it for a second. She liked it. Now all she had to do was get dressed. Emperor told her they were heading out to eat at a local restaurant that doubled as a nightclub to do some dining and dancing. She decided to wear something spectacular, and had just the thing in mind, something Carmena insisted she buy. It wasn't really her style, but Carmena swore to her that she was killin' it when she tried it on in the fashion boutique, so she figured that it'll be the perfect piece to wear.

She went into her walk-in closet and grabbed the dress. A cocaine white and royal satin that was a one-piece, skin-tight, lace-up, made by Saint Laurent. The bodice was strapless, shirred under her breast and skeletal in corset fashion that ended just at her hips, with crisscross laces in the back. Sensual. The remainder of the dress flowed down into a pencil skirt that hugged every one of her curves, with slits on both sides of her thighs, the material ending just at her knees. She had platinum-strapped stiletto heels to add flavor. When she tried it on at the boutique, she couldn't believe how it molded to her curves, lifted her ample breast upward, making her look like she had the strength of a queen. The dress was the bomb. Plus the color fit her perfectly.

She had to admit, Carmena was right. It was as if the dress had been made just for her. She loved it. And she hoped Emperor would too.

Ayana didn't want him to see her until she was ready, but she needed help with the laces, so she called for one of the maids, and one of the ladies was up there in a flash to help her.

Fortunately for her Emperor was busy in the other room and didn't even notice when she let the woman in.

The woman smiled and was more than happy to lace up the back of the corset for her.

Ayana thanked her when she had finished, then sucked in a breath as she surveyed herself in the mirror.

'Yeah, you killin' it, girl," she thought. This dress is the shit!

With her dress laced tight, it molded close to her body, accentuating every curve. She put on a pair of platinum earrings and a Cartier watch, and she was ready.

Opening the door, she found Emperor standing in the living-room, dressed in a black Spanish-design suit with a white no-collar shirt. He was leaning against the arched doorway to the patio, an image of almost divine perfection as he sipped a glass of Agua Luca cachaca. He was fine, and could have been on the cover of any men's fashion magazine. He took her breath away. Maybe they should stay in tonight and just eat away at each other. Her nipples tightened as she stepped into the room. Juices flowing between her legs.

Emperor must have heard her stilettos clicking on the hardwood floor, because his head turned in her direction, eyes lit up.

"Shit, mamacita!"

She warmed under his perusal as he pushed off the wall and came over to her, walked around her, and approvingly nodded his head. "Damn, is that you or the dress?"

She giggled. "Both."

He came around to face her, took her hand, and kissed her fingers. Their eyes locked. "You are truly a beautiful chick, Ayana."

She could feel the thumping of her own heart. "Thanks. You don't look so bad yourself."

With a wide grin, he took her hand and slid it in the crook of his arm. "It took you long enough."

Ayana laughed.

Emperor drove her in his silver and black Rolls Royce Wraith across town to Cartagena's De Caliente, a live Colombian restaurant in Dearborn that contained an upscale nightclub, aligned with yellow, blue, and red spot lights discoing back and forth.

When they pulled up, all eyes were on them. The Wraith had everybody's mouths open in awe, making the atmosphere out Front charged with excitement as people stood in a long line waiting to get inside. Everybody was fresh as hell. Ayana wasn't used to waiting in line. She hoped emperor didn't expect her to, either. That was definitely beneath her. But she would do it, if he asked her to. He had said that it was a pretty exclusive place and there was a dress code, so it wasn't like you could just walk in there and get inside. Your name had to be on the list, which wasn't easy to do at all.

But their names were on the list, thanks to the owner being the father of one of Emperor's soldiers, so they went over to the "reservation" side of the line, and to her delight, walked right in.

Ayana saw that there, were two amazing things right off the rip. There was a tranquil part of the club, and a wild part, which she thought was very unusual, but cool at the same time. even though there was a closed door cutting off the loud music and bar, you could still feel the pounding rhythm vibrating from behind the doors, could see the lights flashing around, and feel the vibe.

As they moved in the opposite direction toward the restaurant and through the doors into soothing music and tables with candle light, Ayana marveled at the amount of funds the owner must have spent on soundproofing the walls, because it was some feat to isolate that thriving rhythm from the ears of the patrons and customers.

It was all dark paneling, cherry woods, and lit up with candles. Romantic. A waiter came by with menus and a wine list. She deferred to Emperor, who ordered a bottle of Sauvignon Blanc. The waiter brought the bottle, poured their glasses, took their food orders, and left them alone.

"I still can't believe how beautiful you look in that dress," he said. "You look like a completely different woman."

"It feels that way, too. I didn't even like this thing when I first saw it. Carmena made me get it. I should be thanking her."

"It wouldn't hurt."

She sipped the wine, loving the sweet, crisp flavor. "I will later."

He shrugged and took a swallow of wine, twirling the liquid around in the glass. "I like being with you. It does something to me. You're very interesting."

"I like being with you, too." She met his gaze. "What?"

"Your face, it's radiant. Your eyes, I never seen any more prettier than yours."

"Bueno," she said, reaching for a wry grin as well as her glass of wine. "You're good. You know exactly what to say, don't you?"

He laughed. "N'all, I just say what I feel, that's all."

Her gaze faded, then came back. "Yeah, you do, don't you? My bad, let me stop."

He reached across the table and laid his hand over hers. "It's all right. You can be yourself with me, Ayana. I want you to be able to say what it is you feel."

"It's like you can see right inside of me. I have never met anyone like you before."

Emperor slid his hand from hers, leaned back in his chair and grabbed his glass. "I would never hurt you, Ayana."

She smiled. "I know that. I can tell by the way you look at me." She caught his smile as he tipped the glass for a drink.

They had made no plans on what would happen with them after they killed Cholo and Ghost. Maybe nothing would happen, and they would go back to living their lives the way they had been before.

Just have fun. Live. Forget about the future for now.

She would. She'd try.

Dinner was a splendid fiesta of sirloin, mouth-watering sauce, and a plate full of delicious garlic fried potato wedges, sided with steamed vegetables. Ayana ate way more than she should have, considering how tight her dress was, but she couldn't resist. It was simply too good a meal.

By the time dinner was finished, they had polished off their bottle of wine. She was stuffed and relaxed.

"Now, let's see if you can dance as well as you eat," Emperor said, pulling her chair out.

Absolutely full, she felt like she was waddling from the restaurant to the dance club in the other room, which she could have found even if she had been blindfolded. She only had to follow the vibration of the thumping bass that led to red velvet ropes attached to brass poles, directing them to wide, rich wood double doors and two oversized bouncers. Emperor gave one of the guys his name, and they were allowed to enter.

Ayana had never seen a club inside a restaurant that had security, and she had been to some fly places in her lifetime. She wondered what was inside that was so special. The doors were held open and they walked in. She was immediately taken back by the flashing bright lights, chest pounding music, and wall-to-wall bodies.

Thankfully, Emperor held her hand, because they hadn't gotten eight feet before the crowd closed in around them from all sides. Good thing she wasn't claustrophobic. The ceiling was lit up with colors of the Colombian flag cascading down from track lighting that seemed to follow them like a spotlight as they made their way through. She would have felt like she was on display if the lights weren't following everybody else, too, in a muted, brilliant yellow, dark blue, and red sort of way. It was live, kind of exciting, almost like colorful beams tracking them. Maybe it focused on body temperatures or something, because everybody's was turned up.

There was a curved bar against the wall, scattered high tables and tall chairs set in front, and the rest of the club was nothing but dance floor, the largest Ayana had ever seen. Good thing too, because that seemed like what everybody was doing up in there -- gyrating to the music. There had to be at least 800 people out there on the soccer field-size floor. The really awesome thing about it was since the dance floor was so enormous, there was plenty of room for everybody to move around without feeling like sardines packed in a can.

"You wanna drink first or dance?" Emperor said, leaning in close to her ear so he wouldn't have to shout.

"I definitely want to dance first. I need to work off some of this food."

He pulled her onto the dance Floor and they made their way out into the crowd. The energy there was contagious and Ayana soon found herself immersed in the music, a sexy Romeo Santos song that had her hips swaying back and forth and raising her arms in the air over her head, turning around and laughing so much her belly ached. She hadn't danced in years, since she was a teenager. Her whole life had changed since then. She rarely had any time to ever enjoy herself anymore. It had been all business.

Emperor was a smooth dancer, he had phenomenal rhythm, and knew how to move his body in a way she found irresistibly sexy, especially when the music slowed to something warm and sensual and he pulled her into his arms. Their bodies touched in all the intimate areas and Ayana lost herself in the music, in Emperor, in the way she felt his embrace. She focused her attention on his hips rocking back and forth with hers, her nipples sliding against his chest, the way his hand pressed against the small of her back, bringing her even closer. She felt his dick against her thigh. It hardened as his eyes turned darker. The room was suddenly smaller, her breaths shorter, and everyone faded away but the two of them, locked in a trance with no words. Yet the dance expressed everything they felt.

He had cast a spell on her. Emperor moved against her body, still in control of the dance, but one hand moved up to press against the side of her neck, his fingers tickling the name as he drew her forward to kiss her. The kiss was a swift, short brushing of his lips against hers. He teased her with the tip of his tongue, no over-dramatic public act of affection, but enough to give her chills and make her wet. Make her want him. She breathed against his lips, letting out a soft sigh.

She knew his plans for the night ended with the dancing at the club, but she didn't want to let him go. She just wanted to be alone with him.

"I'm glad I met you, Ayana," he whispered, releasing her mouth and giving her such an intense stare it forced her to shake.

She nodded, resting her chin on his shoulder so he could hear her. "I'm glad, too. But can we leave now."

He leaned hack, shook his head, and smiled. "Yeah, let's get out of here."

He grabbed her hand and led her out the door. He opened the door of the Rolls Royce for her and she got in.

Instead of taking her home, he decided to take her to a beach nearby. She didn't even question him.

The night was balmy with just the slightest breeze. She slipped her heels off and walked beside him. It was difficult to see anything at all since there was barely a glow of the moon visible in the sky, but that made her other senses activate. She smelled the dense rinse of the river, heard birds chirping calls as they flew overhead. All the night creatures were out. She could still feel the rhythm of the dancing in her soul.

She and Emperor were completely alone out there on the beach. They walked hand in hand just along the water's edge, neither of them saying a word, just enjoying each other.

Once they were out of sight of everything public, he pulled her away from the water, trudging over the sand and underneath a rocky overhang, flipping her around so that her back brushed the craggy stone.

A romantic, passionate kiss told her without a doubt that he wanted her just as much as she wanted him. If there was any part of her that would have rejected fucking him out there in public, it was gone, she wanted him desperately. He lifted one of her legs and held it over his waist, sliding his fingers under the silky fabric to caress the bare skin of her leg. His touch, the clarity in her mind that he desired her this much, sent hot shivers across her skin, making her nipples tingle, her clit quiver, because she wanted him with equal desperation.

Emperor moved his free hand under her thigh and toward her pussy, cupping her, caressing her until she writhed under his touch. He ripped the fabric aside and buried his fingers inside her, pumping her with soft, calculated strokes. She moaned against his mouth and he kissed her harder, relentless in his pursuit and coaxing an orgasm from her that she had no hope of holding back. She pumped against his hand, reaching down to grasp his wrist and hold him there while she shuddered through the currents of pleasure that swamped her. He kept his mouth planted on hers, his tongue like a velvet flame, inducing utters and whimpers, reducing her to a wet, crazed mess.

Ayana finally tore her mouth away from his and reached for his face, cradling his cheeks and forcing him to look at her so she could choke out some breathless words in between her panting. "I want to feel you inside me, papi."

She barely held on while he unzipped his pants, pulled them down, and positioned himself between her legs. He swept one arm around her back and lifted her. With a long groan she sat on his thighs, her toes sliding into the sand as he impaled her pussy onto his dick. Ripples of sensation unleashed inside of her, and she allowed herself to drown in them.

Delicious. Hot. Gripping. Emperor pushed her against the rocks as he began to pump between her legs, his movements grinding his shaft against her already raging and sensitive clit. She had no idea if anyone was walking by looking at them. They were enshrouded in pitch darkness, yet she was far from being quiet as Emperor continued to pound her with merciless, steady thrusts. Her pussy gripping him with tight convulsions. She cried out when he bent his head low and swept her mouth again with a kiss meant to devour, to transform her mind into slush.

After a while, she didn't give a fuck if they had an audience of spectators watching or not, because she only wanted him to continue digging into her. He made her feel fire from her toes to her hair, taking her from one climax to the next. She clung to him in ragged exhaustion and begged him to keep going until he couldn't anymore. He groaned, grinding against her with a wild explosion of his own. She held him tight, feeling all the muscles bulge in his body, dragging her nails over his sweat-soaked back as he shuddered against her, extracting his mouth from hers to kiss her cheek and chin, her neck.

Reality came back to her and she realized where they were.

"You think anybody saw us?" she asked giggling.

"I don't even give a fuck. It was worth it."

She laughed.

They fixed their clothes and Ayana swiped her hand over her hair. "My pussy is still throbbing."

He smirked. "Good," he said, taking her hand. "Because we ain't finished yet. You coming home with me for the night."

Andolian Napraja

Chapter Twenty-One

The temperature was so high it seemed like he was melting. Even though it was night, the heat was unbearable as Juan climbed out the back of the black Mercedes Maybach in front of the Mandalay Bay Casino & Hotel Resort in Las Vegas.

On the strip, a million bright lights flashed from other casinos and billboards everywhere. Onlookers and pedestrians spilled out in all directions, moving aimlessly, photographing moments and unique architectural designs of buildings.

Juan was met at the main entrance by Marc Escobar, his business partner at Galaxy Sports Promotional Inc. there in Las Vegas. Marc had started building GSPI by himself when he was just under Juan's age. He knew the business in and out, and had made millions from it before selling off shares to investors like Juan and their other partner who lived in a remote place in Brazil.

"Marc, it's good to see you," he said, extending his hand for him to shake.

Marc, a slick to the back, dark-hair guy with designer-framed glasses, smiled. "Glad you could make it on such short notice. We have an exciting event coming up in a week. Two championship fights on the same night on two different television networks. It's going to be crazy. We have to get all over this."

They went inside the casino part of the resort and made their way to the UFC arena where there was a small crowd watching a couple fighters spar in the caged ring.

Juan and Marc took a seat in one of the rows and their event manager came over with some papers in his hands. He handed both Juan and Marc a form to read over and sign.

"I just need both of your signatures where the X is on the line at the bottom of the last page. This is for several news conferences and publicity events I have lined up for our lead fighter, Dallace "The Malice" Bucanan."

Juan nodded and signed the paper and Marc did the same. "Well, that was easy. Don't you just love this business," he said.

The event manager walked away.

At the mention of the word "business," Juan's mind drifted for a second, thinking about Cholo and Ghost. In just a couple days, he and Ayana would finally have their revenge. After all the years of their parents being dead, he just couldn't believe that they were going to finally get the people responsible.

Juan tried closing that from his mind and began to focus on why he had come to Las Vegas in the first place, which was to get away from everything and clear his head. But he knew with every second that passed, there was a slight possibility that Cholo, Ghost, and Claudia might either be skipping town or coming after him.

It had been an exhausting two weeks on his mental and emotional stability. He had been chronically paranoid, attentive to everything moving around him. It took everything he had to keep himself together.

After talking with Marc and their project team, he decided to head to his hotel room, where he could be alone and get his thoughts together.

He had reserved a room in one of the resort's Executive Suites. A corporate decorated two bedroom, two-and-a-half bath oceanfront with intracoastal views, featuring an eat-in kitchen, a huge south side party balcony, and a stand-up wet bar. Carpet and marble covered the floors in the entire suite.

The main room consisted of extravagant modern-style furnishing, intentionally positioned in front of the panoramic window.

Juan stepped outside on the balcony and took it all in. Exhaling, he rested his arms on the rail, the cuffs at the ends of his suit jacket breezed in the hot wind. He took the jacket off and placed it on one of chairs behind him.

He closed his eyes and meditated, feeling one with his spirit. He visualized his inner pain and anxiety, saw it as bright as wood burning in a fire in front of him. The dancing of luminous hot flames with shades of red and yellow, stretching from the base, engulfing his entire body from his feet to his head, then to the back of his neck, looping and knotting intricately between his chest and the top of his back.

By picturing the calm, Juan had a clear understanding of whether his sanity was still refined or if it was starting to deteriorate.

Actually, his only concern was how fortified his sanity and morals were.

He was trying hard not to lose himself in the midst of everything, but he was on the verge of snapping.

The pain of losing Brazil had been vicious, it hurt more than the bullet he took when Ghost had shot him. He felt as if a demonic fetus had come alive within him and was clawing its way out.

Fortunately, he had a particularly high tolerance for pain.

After everything he had been through, he had learned to channel and create strength from it all. He was still trying to find some sort of purpose in his life, other than vengeance.

What would he do once Cholo and Ghost were dead? He hadn't known that this was what he had been seeking nearly his whole existence - to find and kill whoever was responsible for murdering his parents when he was a kid.

Juan stepped back into the suite, found the remote to the TV, clicked it on and took a seat on the largest couch in the room.

The Mandalay had the best stations money could buy, but his thoughts were so tied up that he wasn't able to enjoy any of them.

After a while, he just sat there until he ended up nodding off to sleep.

In his dream, he and Brazil were reunited and they were happy, laughing, while making love and rolling around on a white sandy beach somewhere deep on an isolated island off the coast of South America.

It couldn't have been more real. He could feel it, feel her, as if she was right there in his arms. He didn't know it, but in his sleep, he was smiling, and a single tear rolled from his closed eyelid. He was at peace.

Chapter Twenty-Two

Carmena stood outside on the block, listening to Smoke grill one of his soldiers about spending too much money off the package he gave him to sell.

"Nigga, you was only suppose to keep eight thousand out that shit, not ten! What the fuck is you doin'?" he hissed, his voice echoing up the street.

"My bad," the young caramel-complexioned, braided-hair kid said, dressed in a Michael Jordan track suit. "I'll make it up, Smoke, I promise. I just lost track, that's all."

"You damn right, you goin' make it up. That shit ain't free, nigga." His nerves were bad. He didn't really mean to take his frustration out on Lil' Chris, but him doing stupid shit wasn't helping either. He handed him another package of crack, a kilo rocked up and bagged in baggies inside a zip-lock bag. "If you fuck this up, ain't goin' be no more talking, you understand?"

"No doubt. I got you." Lil' Chris gave him a sly grin.

"All right," he said, as he walked back over to Carmena, who was standing with her arms folded.

"I sure hope he handles his business," she said, then exhaled a soft sigh.

"He better hope, too," Smoke said seriously. "I would hate to have a bullet in his young ass."

Lil' Chris started walking up the block, every so often looking back over his shoulder to see if Smoke was still watching him. He was.

Suddenly, a red Durango stopped in the middle of the street down by the corner. Smoke's instincts came alive. They had been beefing with other dealers in the area over territory and sells for the past few months, so he grabbed Carmena by the arm and told her to stand in the doorway of the building, just to be on the safe side. He watched as the driver of the SUV suspiciously sat there and did nothing.

Latrel, one of his soldiers, came up the block, walking from the trap house, looking at him confused.

Smoke shrugged his shoulders, not knowing what was happening.

Two men who had been crouched in the crowd of kids, teenage girls, and crack heads suddenly stood up and walked in front of them with sub-machine guns aimed in Smoke's direction. They started shooting, BLAT-TAT-TAT! BLAT-TAT-TAT-TAT! running up the block. BLAT! BLAT!

The driver of the Durango stepped on the gas, running the Jeep up the street while shooting out the window.

Latrel was hit instantly.

Smoke was forced to watch his little soldier take four slugs to the chest. There was nothing he could do. He turned around and looked at Carmena, making sure she was safe and out of sight. "Stay there. I'll be right back," he told her as he darted to the side of a parked car, pulling a Glock-21 from his waist and firing two calculated shots at one of the two gunmen on foot.

The bullets ripped through the first one's abdomen, sending him towering backward into a tree. The other shooter ducked behind the side of a house.

Smoke waited for the Durango as it sped up the street. As soon as it approached, he ran up and quickly put three in the driver. The jeep dead-rolled, crashing into a fire hydrant, showers of water spraying in the air wildly. He turned around, looking for the other gunmen, but didn't see him.

Where the fuck did this nigga go?

"What's up, now!" he heard a familiar voice say from behind him as he felt a gun being pressed alongside his head, right at his temple. It was Lil' Chris. He told him to turn around and face him.

Smoke turned slow, looking him dead in the eyes, glaring at him.

A devilish smirk appeared on Lil' Chris's face, spread across his lips.

Smoke was steaming. He had always treated Lil' Chris like family. How could he betray him like that?

I should have killed this nigga when I had the chance, he said to himself, frowning hard with his teeth clenched.

Then, from out of nowhere, Carmena appeared from the shadows as if she was some type of angelic spirit sent to protect him. Lil' Chris never heard her creeping up behind up, but he saw the sense of confidence rising in Smoke's eyes. Something told him to turn around, and when he finally did, it was too late. Her moves were swift and lethal at the same time as she launched a switchblade directly into his throat.

Smoke stood there in awe, looking at her with shock written all over his face, not knowing she possessed that type of element inside her, because of the way she portrayed herself. Who would have ever thought...

Astounded and feeling the icy-hot blade penetrate his neck, Lil' Chris grabbed at the knife, choking on his own blood. He dropped to his knees, staring at her with disbelieving eyes as his life began to fade away.

She wiped the blade clean on his shirt and kicked his body over, and just as swiftly as she had pulled it out, she snapped the knife back into its handle and put it away.

"You shouldn't have no more problem out of him," she said with a grin, standing over his remains.

"No, I guess not." Smoke was still stunned. He took her small hand into his and led her over to the cream and almond-colored Flying Spur Bentley parked in front of the building. He opened the door for her, then ran around to the driver's side and got in. With urgency, he hurried up and pulled away as he heard the sirens approaching.

Chapter Twenty-Three

Cholo obviously liked having money. He liked to play, liked to work hard for it, so he didn't have any guilt over where it came from or how he got it. He gave generously to others, to charities and foundations in their efforts to assist the poor and change the world.

He lived a good, prosperous life off the money he made and didn't care how many lives he had to destroy to guarantee his continuous flow of income never ceased. That was the nature of the business.

He and Emilia were preparing themselves in the bedroom for their night at the opera. She tied his tie, straightened his collar to adjust the accessory beneath it, so when she folded it back down, her nails were grazing his hair, the curves on his ears. She had no idea what he was thinking in that head of his, because the only thing on her mind was the taut muscle in his thigh, beneath her bottom. His fingers grazed her back, as if he intended a grip to keep her there. Though she never looked into his face, she felt his regard as if he were branding her flesh, making it is.

A quick tightening, an adjustment of the pin, and she was finished, demonstrating that she was as efficient as she had always been when it came to tying his tie. She rose and passed by his chair.

Cholo stood up and put on his tuxedo jacket, buttoning it.

The limousine was waiting out front. He felt so tense. He wanted to stay home, but he had promised Emilia they would see Sergio Talasias' last performance of his career.

He turned and followed in her direction, down the large hall, looking up at the wall filled with art and paintings. White and black pictures, indigenous artifacts, and old world wooden-carved cultural masks aligned the way to the end.

Emilia was first to be out the door, followed by the five bodyguards. There was no way she was missing Sergio Talasias.

Cholo grunted as he got in the limo after her. The chauffeur closed the door, and they were off.

*****

Standing by one of the front windows in Juan and Ayana's living room, watching as night began to close in over the earth, Emperor plucked handfuls of 9mm ammunition out of the boxes of ammo they had brought from Bugsy's Guns & Supply, and distributed cartridges in the pockets of his suit.

Ayana, Juan, Smoke and Carmena sat around the room loading weapons.

They had over 150 rounds between them. Each one of their weapons contained a screwed-on silent sound suppressor at the end.

Side by side on the sofa, Ayana and Carmena were dressed in cute tailor-made black skirt suits, looking like they were twins, with their hair done flawlessly.

Juan had been quiet ever since he had returned from Las Vegas, but Ayana knew what was on his mind, the same thing that was on hers and everybody else's in the room - killing Cholo.

"Everybody ready?" Smoke said.

Emperor looked around the room, over all their faces. "Remember your positions."

Ayana cocked her weapon. "Let's go get this son of a bitch."

They all spilled out the house, getting into three separate vehicles. Ayana rode with Emperor while Carmena went with Smoke. Juan was the only one to leave solo.

On the same block as rambling structures and office buildings, a federal bank, and a law firm, the Detroit Opera House had fourteen flat steps leading him up to a double set of ten-foot-high oak doors that were recessed in a twenty-foot-high cinquefoil arch, above which was an enormous and elaborately patterned wheel window that still contained two-fifths of its original glass.

The four carved oak doors were weather-beaten, scarred, and cracked. At the center of them, right at the top, beveled letters, cut by a master stone carver, made an assuring statement in the granite lintel, saying "God Lives Through Our Voices."

Hundreds of people had gathered outside, awaiting the grand opening.

"I sure hope y'all right about this nigga showing up," Emperor said to Ayana. They were thick in between the crowd, glancing over all the faces. He had never seen Cholo before, so he didn't have a clue what to look for. "When you spot him, make sure you point him out to me."

"I will. Don't worry," she said, moving beside a fat man that was standing by the entrance.

On the opposite side of the building, off in the distance, Juan was posted in the shadows, barely visible. Leaning against the wall, his eyes scoured over the luxury double-parking vehicles out front and their occupants. Nothing. He checked his watch. The opera show was scheduled to begin in just ten minutes. Cholo should be pulling up at any time now. If he is coming, he figured.

Down on the last step, Smoke and Carmena were almost in plain sight as they stood close to the high-traffic street, their hearts pumping with anticipation. Horns blew from cars as passengers got out. Smoke wondered if they would be able to spot

Cholo in the midst of all the people. "I sure wish I knew how he looked," he said, unsure.

"You'll know soon enough." Carmena locked her arm between his as they started walking toward the end of the block.

As the doors of the opera house opened, Ayana spotted Cholo and his wife, Emilia, getting out of a limousine and heading up the steps, followed by a team of bodyguards. She was pleased to see that Claudia wasn't with them. "Okay, he's here."

"What? Where?" Emperor said, searching through the crowd with his eyes.

She nodded her head, looking directly in front of them. "The older guy with all the bodyguards. That's his wife in the purple dress."

Emperor's eyes fell right on him. "All right, I see him."

Ayana glanced over the crowd, searching for her brother. He was gone. She looked for Smoke and Carmena, but didn't see them either. "Come on, we have to move."

As the spew of people fell into the theater, the entire gang vanished in the crowd.

Juan was one of the last ones inside. He kept a distance from Cholo and his guards, since he would be the first one they'd recognize.

Cholo and his entourage made their way up the grand staircase. Juan followed cautiously.

The stairs led them to a passageway that connected them to the second level. With each step upward, Juan felt his adrenaline begin to rise.

Gripping the rail with his right hand, he could see Ayana and Emperor just head.

When they finally got to the second level, Juan made a hard left and headed for the restroom, just as they had planned. Emperor and Smoke were already inside, waiting for him. Ayana and Carmena were in position in the women's bathroom.

Now all they had to do was wait until the show began.

Cholo had reserved a private box for him and Emilia, the same one he always used. He loved being seated above everyone else. It made him feel like Caesar of Rome. There was something about it that seemed regal.

As Emilia took her seat next to his, all the lights in the theater dimmed, beginning the show.

The opening act consisted of three beautiful Latin women dressed in colorful modern attire appearing from the back of the stage, singing high-pitched sopranos. Each of the ladies wore red scarves on their heads and stood counter-clockwise from one another. The stage theme was set to resemble the kitchen of a middle-class home, while three women gossiped among themselves about their new neighbor, who was so attractive.

Emilia almost melted when she saw Sergio Talasias come in through the side door behind the women, roaring nice and well-delivered baritones. He was magnificent. The ladies began to weep at his presence, as did Emilia, as violin chords, piano keys, and other instruments set the mood in a melodramatic flow.

"BRAVO! SERGIO!" the audience shouted excitedly, giving the musical legend a standing ovation, welcome him. "BRAVO!"

Emperor opened the door and peeped out. The hall was empty, except for Cholo's bodyguards posted outside the door to his booth. He turned around, looking at Juan. "The coast is clear. It's time."

Juan nodded, pulling his gun from the holster on his waist.

Smoke did the same.

Emperor was the first one to walk out the restroom, then Juan, then Smoke, who knocked twice on the door of the women's bathroom to let Ayana and Carmena know that they were moving. Juan and Emperor spread out and allowed Smoke to walk between them to go ahead.

From behind, Smoke could hear the slamming of the woman's bathroom door, which was his signal to open fire on Cholo's security.

But the guards were on point.

As Smoke came up the hall, although they didn't know him from anywhere or had ever seen him before, they instantly knew something wasn't right. One of the guards reached for the gun in his suit jacket, but was struck by a slew of silent slugs.

"OH SHIT!" another one said as he moved to the side. Another hail of bullets whistled through the air, piercing him. He died before his body hit the ground.

Two down, three to go.

Emilia held Cholo's hand tightly as her emotions began to overflow with joy, listening to the soothing voices of Sergio Iglasias harmonize over wonderful melodies of the orchestra, but something else was on Cholo's mind.

"I'll be right back. I'm just going out to the hall to make a phone call."

"But, …"

He waved her off. "Just give me a few minutes…"

She sighed. "Go, just hurry back, please. I don't like sitting in here by myself. It seems unnatural."

He shook his head. Women. They were something else. Always making a big deal out of nothing.

As he pulled the door open an eruption of gunfire exploded in his ears, searing them with loud echoes and screaming whistles. He quickly glanced out into the hall, three of his guards were down, dead, and the last two were engaged in a heated shootout with Juan and two more gunmen he had never seen before, along with Ayana and Carmena.

"FUCK!"

He slammed the door closed.

Emilia stood up. "Cholo, what is it? What's going on out there?"

For the first time in his life, he felt defenseless.

No amount of armory would have made him feel better. He ignored his wife and went into a panic. There was nowhere to run, to hide. He knew if they had got to him this easily, then they would be coming through that door in any minute.

The frightened expression in her husband's face scared the life out of her. He had gone pale. Emilia grabbed him by the shoulders, pleading with him to tell her what was happening.

He stared at her, shock written all over his face, his mouth open, but no words coming out.

More gunfire erupting outside the door.

The music grew louder in the background.

Seconds later, the door swung open. Juan, Emperor, and Ayana walked in, clutching their weapons. Carmena and Smoke stood behind in the hall.

Cholo swallowed hard. "What's... wha... what's this about?" he uttered, staggering over his words, playing stupid.

"Let's see, where do I start..." Juan said. "First, you had my mother and father killed, when me and Ayana were just kids. Then, you turn around and kill my fiancée."

"Who happened to be my sister," Emperor chimed in.

"Um-um-um... Somebody's been a bad boy," Ayana said, laughing.

"Cholo, is this true?" Emilia asked him.

"I did... did you... a favor. That girl was a cop. She would of sent you to prison."

"Don't you dare try to turn this around and play hero. You killed my mother and father in cold blood, and Brazil too. Now it's your time to die..."

"I tried to reason with your fath... with Jose. He wouldn't listen... All he had to do was merge his company with mine and we could of ruled the industry, just as you and I have… Killing him was the last thing I ever wanted to do. And your mother, she wasn't supposed to be there. I'm sorry."

"Yeah, yeah, yeah…" Emperor said, stepping in front of everybody. "Save your apologies, muthafucka!" He raised his gun to his head and, without any hesitation, pulled the trigger, blowing Cholo's brains out the back of his skull.

Juan gave him four more to the chest.

"Noooo!" Emilia screamed. Her voice was muffled by the sound of the orchestra.

"SHUT UP, BITCH!" Emperor yelled, grabbing her by the hair. "Sit the fuck down, before I shoot yo' ass, too!"

She started swinging her arms wildly at him. "YOU SON OF A BITCH! AAAH!"

Ayana sighed, pushing Emperor out of the way. "Move!" She snatched Emilia by the throat with her left hand, and stuck the gun in her face with the other, firing a quick shot right through her open mouth, silencing her. Her body slumped to the floor beside her husband's.

Emperor looked at Juan. "Come on, you ready?"

"Yeah, let's do this."

They holstered their weapons, then reached down and grabbed Cholo's lifeless remains. Picking him up, they tossed his body over the balcony. His corpse fell through the air in slow motion, landing between an older woman in a black dress and a huge, fat man seated in the level below, his head hitting one of the chairs like a thud, cracking the wood in its back from the force, as Sergio Iglasias wrapped up his opening performance, shouting a high and very long baritone that moved the audience.

Emperor smiled. "Now that's what you call a drop-dead performance."

The woman in the black dress let out a horrifying scream, and everybody started running out of the theater in a panic.

It was pure chaos when Smoke opened the door to hall. People were shouting and scattering in all directions, forcing their way down the stairs.

The gang of five came out, stepping over the dead bodyguards, and walked casually away from the booth, blending in with the rest of the crowd.

Andolian Napraja

Chapter Twenty-Four

Detective Ramone Brown was at home working on his computer, going over a recent homicide. It had been a long week of intensive searching for clues and connections surrounding a case involving two young, bisexual girls found floating in the Belle Island River with their hands tied beneath their backs. Some detectives had speculated that the two girls had been slashed across their throats, then tossed over the Belle Island Bridge, but Ramone was starting to believe the girls were killed and maybe thrown off a small passenger boat.

He stared at the photos on the computer screen, which displayed the girls in black body bags after being fished out of the water. He did that a lot - stared at pictures. It was the only way he could get a good read on what might have happened in any of his cases. Pictures were truly worth a thousand words.

Ramone remembered working an old case, and while looking through several photos, he had discovered a wet footprint in the background left on the sidewalk at the murder scene, which ultimately led to the arrest of a construction worker who wore a pair of unique-soled boots to work every day.

That was pure police work.

Out of every detective who had studied the photos, no one had spotted the footprints in the background but him.

Claudia walked in the house and dropped her keys on the dining room table. She moved around, rambling hastily through drawers closets, disturbing him.

Their relationship had begun diminishing months ago, and he had his suspicions that she was seeing someone else, but had not yet verbalized it to her. He had wanted so badly for their relationship to work, but if she wasn't willing to work at it, then there was nothing he could do.

Ramone rose up from the computer and went over to the refrigerator. Reaching on top of it, he grabbed a bag of sour cream potato chips, cracked them open, and poured some in a bowl he got out of the dish-rack. He was getting ready to head back to the computer when his cell phone beeped.

"Detective Ramone Brown," he said, answering it.

"Ramone, I need to see you right away. It's important."

"Ayana? Is everything all right? How's Juan?" he said, surprised to hear from her after a couple months.

"Everything's fine. Juan is okay. But I need your help with something urgent. We don't have much time."

"Okay, where are you?" he asked, hesitatingly.

"At El Miguel's restaurant. You know the place, right?"

"Yeah, I know the place. I'll be there in fifteen minutes."

"See you when you get here."

Claudia had been listening in the other room. She heard everything. She knew he had all sorts of clients, but had no idea Juan and Ayana had been among them.

She waited until Ramone grabbed his coat and was out the door before she decided to follow him.

The sun over the city of Detroit was bright and radiant sitting in the sky.

City cabs, and two buses with loud, heavy diesel-filled engines traveled in opposite directions going east and west as

Ramone parked his car, got out, and walked into El Miguel's restaurant on the busy boulevard of Lafayette.

He couldn't help but wonder what this was all about. He had seen the news and read the three-page article pertaining to the mysterious assassination of Cholo Dominguez and his team of bodyguards gunned down at the Detroit Opera House, and figured that her asking him to meet her urgently had something to do with it. It was just a hunch, but a good one.

She was seated at a window booth, sipping a glass of wine, the bottle in front of her on the table.

Ramone strolled in and took a seat across from her.

"Hey, what's going on?" he said.

"What do you know about Cholo Dominguez?"

"Not much, he's dead now, right? I been following the story on the news and in the papers over the past four days, why?"

"It's not him that I'm interested in. I'm looking for someone else."

He nodded understandingly. "Okay, so what do you want me to do?"

"I want you to see if you can find something on a woman named Claudia Remirez… She was Cholo Dominguez's chief assassin and enforcer."

At the mention of her name, his heart skipped a beat, and quickly began pounding in his chest. "Who did you just say?"

Ayana caught the recognition. "Claudia Remirez. What, you know her?"

"I… I don't… I don't know… I mean, I don't know if it's the same one you're referring to?"

"How do you know your Claudia?"

"Uh… she's… she's my girlfriend," he said, hesitatingly. "We've been together for about a year now. I met her last year when I was shopping at the mall one day. We sort of bumped into each other in the shoe store…"

"Did she ever tell you what she does for a living?"

"Yeah, but it certainly wasn't killing. She said she was Senior Director of Millennium Real Estate International." As soon as it came out of his mouth he realized what he'd just said. He had recently read the article on Cholo Dominguez and the on-going conspiracy of Millennium Real Estate International, the awful murders and infamous schemes behind its rise to corner the real estate industry in Michigan. "It can't be… my… my Claudia…" he said, unbelieving.

"Listen, I know it's hard to believe, but I can't lie, Ramone, it sounds just like the same person to me. Do you have a picture of her or something you can show me?"

"As a matter of fact, I do." He reached in his pocket and pulled out his wallet, he opened it and there was a small rectangular photo of him and Claudia hugging each other as they sat in the grass at an amusement park of some kind. Nothing about her was different, she even had the same red hair, only it was shorter now. They looked happy together.

"Yeah, that's definitely her."

"Are you sure?"

"I know her real well, Ramone. We have a long history. We've done things together. I'd recognize her anywhere."

Ramone felt like a fool. Stupid. He had no idea. Him being a cop and all, he was supposed to have instincts. Instincts that told him things. She had pulled wool so far over his eyes, he just couldn't believe he had been so naive.

Usually, in the beginning of his relationships, he would do a thorough background check on his girlfriends, and their family, to be sure they were who they appeared to be, but with Claudia it had been different. It just never crossed his mind. An assassin… he thought, how in the hell did I not see that?

"Ramone, I need to know how to find her," Ayana said, bringing him out of his trance.

He shook his head. "I can't… I can't give her to you."

She leaned forward, closer to him, her hand now on top of his. "Ramone, she murdered my mother and father. I need to know how to find her…"

"I can't, Ayana. You don't understand… our relationship has been on rocky ground for some time now. She's been living somewhere else. I don't have any idea how to get in touch with her."

"When was the last time you seen her?"

"Just minutes ago, she was at my house, probably packing some things, but you can bet she's not there anymore. She hasn't stayed there for over two months now. She'll come by and grab a few things, but she never stays."

*****

Just on the other side of the street, hidden in the shadows between two buildings in a dark alley, Claudia never missed a beat. She had seen everything. She couldn't believe he had the nerve to show Ayana the picture they had taken at Cedar Point. That was supposed to be something special between the two of them. Something personal and intimate. She knew they were having problems, but she would never had sold him out had the roles been switched and Ayana was asking her the questions. How could he? She was burning inside, death was in her eyes. That son of a bitch…

It was like a nightmare. Ramone felt sick to his stomach. All he wanted to do was get out of there. He felt small, insignificant, like he had been a pawn.

Breath came to him suddenly, implosively. The paralysis broke with a spasm that nearly shook him from head to toe.

He looked at Ayana sitting in front of him, afraid he had said too much. Afraid that she would be watching his home, expecting to catch Claudia.

He got up, sat a tip on the table for the waitress, and began walking away without another word.

Ayana didn't bother calling his name, she just let him go.

He staggered outside, hoping the fresh air would relieve him somehow, but it didn't. It was too hot outside, the heat only made his anxiety worse than it had been. If he didn't get to his car soon, he was going to faint.

It was just a few feet away, but his moves were slow, as if he was trapped in a dream-like trance, gradually being pulled by a gravitational force into another dimension.

One foot in front of the other, each step seemed like it was minutes apart.

He made it in the street, and around the door, his hand tugged at the handle.

His keys… Where are the keys… He reached in his pocket, felt them.

Almost there now.

He pulled the keys out, found the right one and slipped it into the keyhole. The lock popped. Suddenly, he saw a shadow emerge from behind him. He turned around, and there she was, his love, the woman who had tricked him out his heart, the assassin. Claudia. Her face was brimstone like the sight of Satan, eyes flaming red, and he swore he could see smoke misting out her mouth as if she was breathing fire.

"Claudia…" he uttered in a daze. "What are you doing here?"

"I saw you with her, Ramone. What have you told her?"

"Nothing. I haven't told her anything."

"I saw you show her a picture of me. That didn't look like nothing to me."

"She wanted me to tell her where you were, but I told her I didn't know… She said you were an assassin, is that true, Claudia?"

She smirked. "Really, you're so pathetic, Ramone... You had to be under some sort of rock or something, how could you not know... I mean, it was in the papers and everything years ago. That's like not knowing who John Gotti was, or Griselda Blanco."

"So, you're admitting you're an assassin?" His eyes were studying hers.

"I do what I'm best at. It's nothing personal, Ramone."

At that, she revealed to him a silver .380 auto.

"You cold-hearted bitch!" he said angrily, feeling betrayed. "You're going to burn in hell for everything you've done."

Ha! Ha! Ha! She burst out laughing at him. "You're probably right," she said, her eyes as cold as ice. "But until then, I'm going to reign on Earth." Claudia lifted the .380 and popped him twice in the forehead.

*****

The loud disturbing noise got Ayana's attention immediately.

A small crowd had begun to form outside the window, the waiters inside the restaurant ran out the door, eager to see what was going on.

Ayana curiously followed behind them.

When she got outside, to the left of the restaurant, she saw that Ramone's car was still parked out front. The mob of people standing around seemed to be looking at something on the ground just beside it. Some women looked on in amazement, covering their mouths with their hands, horrified at the sight.

Ayana moved closer to get a look for herself.

As she approached the back of the crowd, between people, she could see Ramone lying in the street, dead, two holes sat in the center of his forehead almost perfectly.

She glanced over the bevy of faces surrounding him. Nobody looked familiar. But when she turned around, she instantly caught sight of Claudia Remirez slowly driving past the scene in a black 7-Series BMW.

Their eyes locked for a second, then Claudia sped away laughing.

Chapter Twenty-Five

The Only way we're going to find Claudia now, or Ghost, for that matter, is if we catch either of them at Cholo's old house…" Juan said, after Ayana had informed him about what happened at the restaurant with Ramone. "Cholo's estate is going to be handed down to Ghost, and all his other properties, businesses, and endeavors, too. Technically, he's our partner, now that Cholo's gone."

"You're right." Emperor agreed.

The entire gang were all seated around the breakfast table by the pool at Emperor's house in Bloomfield Hills.

"They won't he expecting that." Emperor said finishing his statement.

"So how do we do it?" Carmena stated the obvious. "There's going to be a lot more security to get through than at the opera house, which could mean it's a lot more dangerous."

"Well, we just can't sit back and do nothing. We have to get them before they get us… You better believe Ghost is not going to let what happened to his father go," Juan stated.

"We don't have a choice, we have to get him at the house." Emperor said.

"What about Claudia? How do we get her? I mean, what if she's not there? Then what do we do?" Carmena asked.

"We will have to find another way to get later. But, for right now, let's just focus on getting Ghost out the way," Ayana said.

She looked around the room, everybdoy was shaking their heads in agreement.

"Then it's settled…" Carmena said. "We go after Ghost."

*****

The black Bell Jet Ranger executive helicopter conveyed Ghost to his parents' home out in Troy, Michigan, and landed on the black-top circular helipad in the backyard. With black calfskin seats, brass fixtures and cabin-walled interior plushly upholstered in emerald-green reptile skin, the ambiance was even more luxurious than in the passenger compartment of a Lear jet. The chopper offered a more exquisite selection of liquor and drinks than what was available on his father's plane, including bottles of Francios Rebelious.

His flight seemed longer than what it really was, he had drank three glasses of Remy XO, trying to clear his mind. He still couldn't believe his parents were gone. And to think that, it was all his fault. He had underestimated Juan and Ayana. His father had warned him, he should have listened. His action had not only caused the death of his father, but his mother as well. She had been innocent in the whole ordeal, not knowing the evils her husband and son had done.

Ghost was met at the landing spot by Padrino Diaz, who had been Cholo's chief of security at the house. Padrino was about forty-five years old, a hundred and eighty pounds, with brush-cut salt-and-pepper hair. His face was all hard planes, and his eyes were sunken behind sunglasses even though the sky was overcast. He wore combat boots, khaki slacks, a tan shirt, and a battered leather flight jacket with numerous zippered pockets. His vertical posture, disciplined manner, and clipped speech pegged him for a retired army sergeant who was unwilling to change the attitude, habits or wardrobe of a military careerist.

"Welcome home, Mr. Dominguez!" Padrino shouted as the wind from the helicopter blades blew over them harshly.

"Ghost, please, call me Ghost... I'm not my father!" he said, and then realized how true that was. He wasn't his father, he didn't possess his father's patience and cunning, his intelligence.

Ghost carried a black briefcase into the house and went into one of the rooms that flanked the living room. He emptied the contents on the king-size mattress, took off his designer glasses, placed them on the bed, then examined all the documentation that proved him to be the heir of his father's empire.

Any other time, he would have been feeling good, ready to celebrate his success, but he had a number of things to work on first, including how he was going to kill his enemies in the most efficient way.

After a couple minutes, he put on his glasses and went out into the living room. He interrupted Padrino's television viewing of the news. "We don't sleep until those muthafuckas is dead, you understand?" he ordered.

"I'll let everyone know," Padrino said. "The compound is already on lockdown."

"Good."

He left the room and strolled down the hall to his father's office. He walked in and closed the door behind him. His father's desk, usually occupied with scattered papers and open books, was now neat and concise, seemingly dreadful. Ghost rubbed his hand over the expensive polished wood surface as he made his way over to the stereo encased in the customized glass and wood-paneled cabinet. He opened the glass door, then hit "PLAY". A song by Marc Anthony came on. He let the Spanish instruments and the message of words envelop him, feeling it in his soul. At that moment, he became his father. He took a seat behind the desk in the massive chair that he used to watch Cholo hand down so many orders in, and reclined all the way back, closing his eyes.

*****

It was 9:55 p.m. when Smoke pulled to the curb down the street from the huge mansion and parked. Carmena had been quiet the entire ride. Smoke wondered if something was bothering her, but he never asked. He just allowed her to have some solitude.

She was trying to stay focused and keep her mind on the mission, but today would have been her father's birthday, if he wasn't dead. Sometimes, she wished things wouldn't have turned out the way that they did between him and her mother. She could still remember that day when he came home to confront Mena, her mother, about what she had done.

"MENA!" he yelled, as he came through the door of their two-story home. Tears were in his eyes, and he was moving around angrily, pacing back and forth.

"What's wrong, daddy?" Carmena had asked him.

He looked down at her sitting at the dining room table doing her homework, and more tears followed.

At that very moment, she knew he had found out about her and her mother's big secret.

Carmelo picked her 13-year-old frame up and held her in his arms, squeezing her tighter than he had ever done before. "I'm not going to let nothing happen to you no more…" he told her, whispering in her ear. "You hear me."

Stunned, Carmena just nodded. "Don't hurt mama, daddy. She didn't mean it …"

He sat her down, and his eyes suddenly went cold.

Behind Carmena, Mena stood in the doorway. She and Carmelo's eyes were locked on each other.

"BITCH, YOU LET THEM NIGGAS UP THE STREET RUN A TRAIN ON OUR THIRTEEN-YEAR-OLD DAUGHTER, SO YOU CAN GET SOME FREE CRACK? WHAT THE FUCK IS WRONG WITH YOU?" His voice caterwauled through the house as he walked towards her slowly.

That's when Carmena saw it - a long, rugged knife with a black handle clutched in his hand.

Her mother got one good look at that thing, then took off running out the house. Carmelo was right behind her.

"NOOOOO, DADDY! NOOOOO!" Carmena screamed, but her father never looked back. His mind wasn't there, he was too far gone in a deadly trance and wouldn't come out of it until her mother was dead. Only the beast inside him remained.

Around thirty minutes later, Carmelo returned back to the house without Mena, blood all over his shirt and pants, the knife still in his hand.

"Daddy, where's mama? What did you do?" Carmena cried. "Noooo, daddy, noooo! You didn't..." Tears poured from her young eyes. It was the hardest thing she had ever felt. The pain was too much for her to bare. "Why, daddy? Why?"

Carmelo stood in the center of the floor, staring at her, his eyes wild. He said, "I love you, Carmena... I'm sorry, baby! I'm sorry, baby. I'm so sorry..." He dropped the knife on the floor, backed away, turned, then walked out the door, never looking back.

"Daddy, come back!" she cried, but he was gone.

That was the last time she saw either of her parents alive. She wept for a whole week straight when his body had been found in an alley. Her whole life had changed after that, making her cold. Even though her mother had been wrong for what she had done to her, soliciting her for sex, Carmena still loved her mother and knew she wasn't in her right mind. The drugs had diluted her judgement and reasoning.

Now, in the passenger seat of the car with Smoke, Carmena considered telling him the secret she had kept buried in her heart for so many years. She wondered how he would respond. Would he judge her?

With that in mind, she dismissed the thought from her head, figuring he would never understand. No one would, not even her cousins, which was why she had never told either of them that Carmelo had been her father, and he was only trying to protect her when he killed her mother.

"You good, baby?" Smoke asked, looking at her with concern. He had noticed that she had drifted off for a minute, but didn't want to interrupt.

"Yeah, just thinking. That's all," she replied flatly.

"Good, but baby, I need you focused. We need to make sure we watch everything. We can't afford any surprises."

She let out a sigh, then sat up in her seat. He was right, she needed to get focused. This was a very serious moment. "All right, I got you."

Satisfied, Smoke went back to staring straight ahead at the massive house, and the guards that frequented around it.

*****

Shortly after dark, Emperor, Ayana, and Juan all sat on the opposite side of the house from where Smoke and Carmena were. Juan studied it from the backseat. Nothing seemed threatening or unusual to him, but what was? He felt that he no longer knew the world that he lived in, that it was unfamiliar to him. Everything that he thought he knew was a lie, the ones he had once called his friends and his partners had been his ultimate enemies, pretending that they had his best interests at heart, just stringing him along for the ride until the one day they decided they were finished with him.

He had gotten Brazil killed by trying to walk away from the business, revealing his hand to his enemies, but how was he supposed to know they were pretending? How was he supposed to know they were conspiring against him? How was he supposed to know that Cholo and Ghost had been father and son? How was he supposed to know Cholo had ordered the murders of his mother and father all those years ago? He couldn't. There was no way of knowing, and that was what bothered him the most.

"I see somebody…" Anaya said, pulling him out of his trance.

Juan focused in on the window of the house.

Emperor shifted his position, now leaning against the door with his hand under the steering wheel, staring straight ahead. He could see directly inside the house, its lights on all through it. A man standing in the corner window was keeping watch.

From where they were sitting in the car, the man looked to be some sort of military personnel, probably a hired mercenary. Emperor could tell by the way he was positioned in the window, looking through a pair of binoculars, his legs spread apart.

Every time the man seemed to be looking at them, Emperor made an abrupt movement to gain his attention. This last time he did it, it seemed to have gotten the job done. He could see the man summon another man to the window to join him. Then, without hesitation, the first man pointed out the window at them, sitting in the car, and then the other man walked away quickly. Emperor would bet his last dollar that he was on his way out there to see who was in the car.

"Well, it's about time," he said. "I'll call Smoke and Carmena to let them know."

*****

Padrino stood at the window, holding the pair of binoculars. Out of curiosity, he sent two guards to check out a car that was parked not too far from the house. He could have sworn that he had seen a movement inside it. There had to be someone in it, watching the house.

Figuring it could only be news reporters, he sent the guards to send them away. There was too much going on, and they didn't need the publicity or the paranoia. Ever since Ghost had arrived, he had been on the edge. Cholo had made him feel the same way just days before he had been killed.

Padrino stepped away from the window and sat down in the chair at the dining room table. He pulled out a walkie-talkie and patiently waited to receive word back from the two guards that everything was fine.

Sal and Davie made their way out the back door of the house, creeping around to the side where Padrino had pointed to the parked car along the street. Sal thought it best to come around behind the vehicle. That way, it would throw whoever was in it off guard and frighten them.

"Wait up, Sal," Davie said, as they light-stepped through bushes and brush leading to the main gate.

"Shut up and just keep an eye out," Sal opened the gate at the entrance point. It squeaked at the hinges, but they continued on through. The car, a black Jaguar, sat just in front of them, about three feet away. Sal gave Davie a nod, and they pulled their weapons out.

Once they were close enough, Sal ran up on the passenger side window. "DON'T MOVE!" he shouted, but to both of their surprises, the car was empty.

"Ah, what the hell?" David said in a whiney voice. "What type of shit is Padrino on? I'm not in the mood for jokes... There's nobody here!"

Sal could have sworn he had seen somebody as well when Padrino pointed the car out to him from the window.

Unsure what was going on, he stood in front of the car and stared at it for a minute. That's when he noticed the reflection from the tree moving on the windshield, perhaps that's what they had seen, he concluded. It had to be. Padrino pulled out his walkie-talkie and called it in. He and Davie headed back to the house.

"Fuckin' Padrino!" Davie said, still feeling like they got played. "I was in the middle of a good nap, too," he said, as they went back through the gate.

*****

It would have been pitch-black outside, except the house had so many lights around it that it made it hard for the team of three to maneuver. The only thing in their favor was the fact that the property was almost covered in trees and tall bushes, which provided them enough cover to get where they needed to be.

They stopped beside a large tree, Ayana was getting ready to move again, but Emperor grabbed her arm, then pointed. The two guards who had come out to check the car were returning to the house, unknowingly, only two or three feet away, they walked right past.

Once they were out of sight, Ayana made her move. Emperor and Juan followed closely behind. They arrived at the guard post at the front gate. Three guards were seated inside, two behind a small table, the other one standing at the other end by the window.

Ayana gave Emperor and Juan a nod, assuring they were ready.

Emperor nodded back at her first, then Juan.

The three of them lifted their weapons and, without warning, fired multiple rounds into the post, ambushing the guards with a hail of bullets.

Two of the guards died, never knowing what hit them, never hearing the shots from the silent suppressors on their attackers' weapons.

When she was convinced they were all dead, Ayana opened the door to the guard post and clicked the lights off so no one could see them.

One of the guards was still breathing, scrambling around on the floor.

She went over and gave him a quick shot to the head, then walked out and pulled the door back shut.

Emperor pulled out his phone and dialed Smoke's number. He let it ring twice, then hung up, signaling to him and Carmena that they were in.

It was time for them to split up like they had agreed to do back at the car. There were simply too many guards on the compound, they would easily be spotted if they all stayed together.

Ayana was the first to break from the pack. "I'm going this way…" she whispered to Emperor, then looked at Juan. "I'll meet up with y'all once we get in the house. Keep y'all eyes open. They can discover those guards' bodies at any time, and all hell could break loose." She kissed Emperor on the lips and hugged her brother. "You two, be safe."

"You too," Emperor said, and she was gone, disappearing into the night.

"I'm going to go around back," Juan said.

"All right, I guess I'll take the side then. "

They both seemed to let out a sigh, looking at each other, unsurely.

"You be careful," Juan told him.

"Don't worry, I got this… You just stay on point."

Juan nodded, then dipped off into the wooden area. Emperor stood there and watched him for a second, hoping he would be okay, then he took off running in the opposite direction.

*****

Juan was the first one to gain entry to the house. He walked through it, cautiously making his way to the kitchen. He could make out the sound of two men having a conversation, one of their voices resembled one of the guards who had been sent outside to check the car. He was sure it was the same guy, he could tell by the way he whined when he talked.

The voices were coming from just on the other side of the wall. Juan inhaled a deep breath, then exhaled strongly as he spun around the corner and fired two quick shots at the first person he saw.

*****

Ayana scanned through the windows outside the house, looking inside to see if she could spot what room Ghost or Claudia were in.

The good thing about being outside in the dark was nobody inside a room could see you, because the light in the room would only reflect off the window and provide a mirror of the images inside the house, preventing the person outside from being detected, which gave Ayana the perfect camouflage.

Not spotting Ghost or Claudia in any of the rooms, she moved on.

*****

Believe it or not, Emperor climbed one of the trees to reach the open window upstairs. He pushed the window all the way open, then lightly jumped to the edge, holding his body up by his hands, hanging at the side of the house.

After a few adjustments, he pulled himself in and quietly crept over to the bedroom door to peep out in the hall.

The Glock-21 in his hand, he cracked the door and locked out. The hall was clear.

He stepped out into the hall, tracing the carpet with light steps.

Cautiously, he stopped at every room, familiarizing himself with the overall layout of the second floor, before making his way downstairs where it seemed that everybody in the house was.

*****

PUTE! PUTE! PUTE!

The two guards standing at the bar with two drinks in their hands fell to the floor. Juan's heart was beating rapidly. He spotted a closet just behind them and hurried to get their bodies into it.

Dragging them one by one, he stuffed them inside, then closed the door.

Just as he was about to continue on down one of the hallways, he heard a crack in the stairs behind him, and quickly turned around, firing two quick shots. PUTE! PUTE!

Emperor ducked and ran, dodging both bullets.

"Oh shit!" Juan whispered, nervous as hell." "My bad, bro!"

Emperor gave him a skeptical look, then shook his head understandingly. He knew the tension was high. There were so many guards around it was giving him the jitters too.

They decided it was better that they now stay together to watch each other's backs. Juan led the way down the hell while Emperor walked backwards, making sure no one got behind them.

The first room they went by the door was closed, neither of them bothered to check inside to see if anyone happened to be in there, they just continued on. But once Emperor had moved about a foot past the door, it suddenly opened, and out came a guard. He spotted Emperor and Juan on the other side of him.

Before he could pull his weapon, Emperor put one in the guard's head, dropping him instantly. "Fuck!"

He glanced back at Juan and nodded, telling him to continue on while he took care of the body.

Juan nodded back and kept moving.

The final bedroom at the end of the hall, which puts him on the west wing of the house, had a rather large dark-wooden door. He could hear the sound of Marc Anthony playing on the stereo just on the other side of it.

Calculating his next move, he turned and took a glance down the hall, looking for Emperor.

At first, he didn't see him, but then he appeared from around the corner. Juan gave him the nod that someone was inside the room. Emperor eased his way up and examined the massive door. He understood why Juan had picked this one to stop at. It was massive in size and elegant, probably an office. If he had to bet, he would bet that Ghost was on the other side of it with his feet kicked up, listening to the radio.

Without further hesitation, Juan put his hand on the door handle and turned it, then pushed the door open.

*****

Claudia Remirez pulled up to the entry point of the guard post, flashing her high-beams. She waited for a second but no one came out to let her in, which she found strange.

She clicked her headlights off, then got out of the car and walked over to the post to have a look inside.

Instantly, she saw the three guards lying dead on the ground. Claudia reached her hand inside the post and hit the alarm button on the wall. The siren came alive over the entire compound, slowly winding like the sound of a prison escape, blaring loudly in the air.

She reached her hand through the window of the car door, pulled her small .380 auto from her purse, then tossed the purse back on the seat as several guards poured out of the house and other areas, running toward her at the post.

"What's going on?" Padrino asked her, making his way through the crowd of men.

"Intruders!" she yelled. "We have intruders! Search the compound!"

Padrino took a look inside the post. "Shit!"

*****

Ayana cursed as the alarm sounded. She hadn't even made out what room Ghost was in yet. She knew time wasn't on her side and she needed to get out of sight before she was spotted.

As she was about to retreat and head in another direction, she spotted Juan and Emperor through the last window, and sitting back in a large chair behind the desk was none other than Ghost. Ayana examined the picture-view window. She considered crashing through it.

All, what the hell... she thought. What do you have to lose?

Without further deliberation, she exhaled, backed up, and just as she was about to run and crash through it, three guards appeared from out of nowhere, opening fire on her. BOOM! BOOM! BOOM!

"SHIT!" She turned and dashed the other way.

*****

Smoke and Carmena were in the gigantic parking garage where Cholo had kept his car collection when the alarm started. "All right, our cover's blown," Smoke said. "It's all or nothing now. Make sure you stay close to me."

Carmena loved that he was always trying to protect her. That was something new to her. She thought it was sexy to have a man that seemed to care about her the way he did.

Smoke opened the rear door to the garage and was instantly spotted by two guards who happened to be running toward the house. He dropped low to the ground and fired several rounds.

Carmena followed suit, darting to the side. PUTE! PUTE!

The guards returning gunfire. BOOM! BOOM!

POP! POP! POP!

BOOM! BOOM! BOOM!

PUTE! PUTE! PUTE!

It seemed like it went on forever. Smoke aimed high, rolling around on the ground. To his delight, he caught one of them in the abdomen, he fell backwards into the arms of the other guard.

That was all she needed to see, like a spider watching its prey get caught in her web, Carmena moved swiftly with utter concentration and sent two meditated shots to the remaining guard's head. His body dropped to the ground fast and hard like he had been clotheslined.

Smoke got up off the ground with a smirk on his face. "If you keep saving my life, I'm going to owe you my eternity in hell."

She laughed as they took off running.

*****

Leaning forward, Ghost's darkened eyes studied Juan's and occasionally checked out Emperor's, too. He smiled. "Fellas, what can I do for you?" he asked humorously, before dashing from the chair, quickly letting off a ruffle of shots at them, shooting at them sideways, he disappeared through the conjoining doors.

"SON OF A BITCH!" Juan said, not believing how quick he was.

*****

Claudia walked through the front door, followed by an army of guards. She took a quick glance around the living room, then she heard a bump somewhere near the west wing. "Everybody split up! Find them and kill em'!" she barked.

The guards took off in all directions, leaving her standing by the door by herself. She stood there and listening for a minute, trying to detect the direct area from which the bump had originated.

After several seconds of deliberation, she decided to head down the west wing's bottom-floor hall.

*****

Padrino was a hound dog, he could smell the scent of intruders from a mile away.

Following his instincts, he traced a scent to the side door entrance of the house. The more steps he took, the stronger the scent grew. It was a feminine aroma, that he was sure of.

He came through the kitchen, expecting to catch someone off guard, but was surprised to find that no one was there.

Confused, he turned around. WHAMM. Something slammed him across the side of his face, hitting him so hard it brought him down to his knees.

WHAMM! Another blow to the face. He put his hands up to try to block the next one, still not able to see his attacker.

Fog-eyed from the impact, Padrino could only make out two things; the fact that his attacker was a female; and in her hand was a switchblade.

With skillful speed, the female assailant twisted the blade fast in her hand and launched it right in his throat.

As his vision grew dark, he could see this woman quickly tuck the blade back into its handle, then put it away. A smile appeared across her lips as she stared at him sideways. Blood rushed from his neck, soaking his clothes as the oxygen from his lungs left his body.

The last thing he saw before he died was the woman kiss a man who had been leaning off to the side, enjoying the playful charade of cat and mouse.

*****

Juan and Emperor darted through the conjoining door, searching for Ghost, but they came up short. Once again, he had vanished.

The door in the second room that led to the hallway was wide open.

Juan ran toward it.

"WAIT!" Emperor shouted from behind him as he saw Ghost appear from the window curtains.

PUTE! PUTE! PUTE!

The three rapid shots caught everybody off guard, including Ghost, who took all three in the back.

PUTE! PUTE! More shots followed.

Ghost fell forward against the wall, forcing the window curtains to fall down on him, covering half his body.

That's when Juan and Emperor saw Ayana standing on the other side of the window with her gun in her hand. A sense of relief on her face.

Then suddenly, her expression changed.

When Juan and Emperor turned around, Claudia Remirez stood in the doorway with her gun trained on them.

Not the one to hesitate, she fired two quick bursts into Juan's abdomen, since he was the closest one to her.

"NOOOOO! JUAN!" Ayana screamed frantically, before running and crashing through the window, shooting wildly, shattering glass everywhere.

Emperor let off a couple rounds of his own while he took cover behind the conjoining door.

Claudia was outnumbered. She backed into the hallway and was instantly hit from the side by a round of unexpected gunfire that slammed her against the wall. She turned her head and saw Carmena running toward her with a guy she had never seen before, both shooting at her.

With all the strength she had left, she picked herself up and returned a rain of bullets toward her attackers, then struggled to run up the hall.

Ayana was on her heels, PUTE! PUTE! Not wanting to allow her to get away. But she was quick, and as soon as she turned the corner, Ayana was met by a team of security guards, rushing their way. "Shit!" She spun around, running back in the other direction.

Time was running out, they had to get out of there. Ayana ran back into the room. Smoke and Emperor had grabbed Juan. He was on his feet but hurt very badly. They dragged him out the same window that Ayana had crashed through, and Ayana set the curtains ablaze to cut off the guards' exit point. They would have to go all the way around to the other side of the house to be able to get to them, and by that time, they would be gone.

Emperor and Smoke held Juan's arms over their shoulders as they ushered him to the car. With no time to get to the other vehicle, they were all forced to pile into the Jaguar.

As they sped away, all the guards were just starting to pour out the house behind them, but they were too late. Emperor spun the car around the corner and they disappeared into the night.

In the car, Juan was starting to go cold, his body was shaking. Ayana sat in the backseat with him and Carmena. She held his hand in hers.

"We… we did it… sis. We… got him…" he struggled to say.

"Just hold on, Juan. We're going to get you to the hospital…" she said, tears falling from her eyes uncontrollably.

"I'm not going to make it to the hospital, sis. I can feel it… It's over. But I'm good now… I can see Brazil waiting for me…" He reached his hand out as if he was touching someone, but nobody was there.

"Juan, don't talk like that… Hurry up, Emperor!" she screamed.

Emperor was stepping on it. They were flying down the intersection, passing by every car in the lanes.

"Don't let that bitch get away, Ayana… I love you, sis…" Those were his last words. He squeezed her hand tight, then he was gone. She could actually hear his soul leave from his body.

"JUAN!" she screamed. "JUAN, DON'T LEAVE ME!" She sobbed, shaking his body, looking for some type of response. But he wasn't there, his spirit had ascended.

Andolian Napraja

Chapter Twenty-Six

Claudia held her arm as she hurried into the safe house in a rush to patch up her wound. She ran to the bathroom and grabbed her kit, then quickly carried it to the kitchen.

At that second, she thanked God for all of her training and felt blessed she knew what to do in this type of situation. Most people would panic, but not her. She knew exactly what to do.

She pulled a knife out of the drawer, turned the stove on, and placed over the fire.

While it heated, she ripped her shirt off and examined the wound. There was a large hole in the mid-section of her arm, where it folded near the muscle.

Taking some alcohol out of the kit, she drenched it over the area. "Ahhhhh!" It was agonizing, but absolutely necessary. She had to stop the bleeding.

With no other option, she grabbed the knife off the stove, took a deep breath, then placed it on her arm. "Ahhhhhhh!" The pain was more excruciating than anything she had ever felt. When she removed the knife, the wound had ceased bleeding on one side. Now all she had to do was stop the bleeding from the exit point.

Claudia sat the knife back on the stove, then repeated the same procedure. "OOOOOOH… GOD! DAMN, THIS SHIT HURTS!" she exhaled harshly, then dropped to the floor, the knife still in her hand. The hard part was over. All she had to do now was patch herself up.

Once she had finished, she hopped in the shower, washed all the blood off, then got out and threw on a red bathrobe and some house shoes.

Fuck! She couldn't believe Ghost was dead. If only she had gotten there seconds earlier, she could have prevented it. For the first time in her life, Claudia felt alone. Cholo had been like a father to her, now he was dead. She and Ghost had been growing close, but now that was cut short, too.

Faced with immeasurable odds and adversity, Claudia knew it was time for her to disappear for a while. She had to go and rebuild her life. For a second, she thought of Ramone. A shame how their relationship ended. She always knew she was going to break it off with him one day, but she never expected it to be that way.

Oh well... she thought. You live and you learn.

She moved through the house, gathering a few things to take with her on her trip. She figured she would head down to Miami to lay low for a while.

Tossing everything she needed in a large suitcase, Claudia was ready to head out.

As she picked up the suitcase, she could have sworn she heard a sound outside near the front door.

There it was again, a thud against the door.

She knew she had been watching her mirrors the whole time she was driving. It was impossible that somebody had followed her.

Another sound.

Without further hesitation, Claudia went straight into war mode. She darted into the bedroom and grabbed the AR-15 from under the bed. It was already loaded. She racked it, then quickly ran back to the living room.

Someone was messing with the door.

"MUTHAFUCKAS!" she screamed, pulling the trigger. BLAT! BLAT! BLAT! BLAT! Slugs pierced through the front door window, shattering the glass into pieces.

She waited for a second, listening for footsteps or some sort of sign of deception.

"CLAUDIA! WAIT! DON'T SHOOT! IT'S ME!" someone said, taking a peek through the broken window. "GHOST!"

"GHOST?" she shouted unbelievingly.

"Yeah, it's me, baby!" he said, sticking his hand through the window to turn the knob on the door.

Claudia was stunned. She couldn't believe he was still alive. "But how? I thought you were ..."

"What, dead?" he laughed. "Don't you just love magic tricks?"

She shook her head, confused. "How did you survive? How are you not dead? I saw you ..."

"The vest, baby. You know I stay with the vest on." He opened his shirt and showed it to her, then turned around so she could see the bullet holes scattered over the back. "When that bitch shot me, I just laid there and played dead. I figured after it was all over, they'd forget about me, and I was right. The bullets didn't even penetrate this time."

Claudia couldn't help herself. She burst into a roar of laughter. Only Ghost could pull something like that off.

He looked over in the corner and saw her suitcase on the floor. "Going somewhere?"

"Yeah," she said. "I think we should disappear for a while, until things cool off." She hoped he would understand and wouldn't fight her about it, or try talking her into staying. She knew the stakes were too high at the moment. Luck wasn't on their side.

"Okay," he finally said. "Let's go." Claudia smiled, happy that he had made the right decision without an argument. I knew he was the one, she thought.

That night, they boarded Cholo's old jet, and were on a flight to Miami, where the weather was a lot better, and the opportunities were limitless. And more importantly, where they had no enemies. Neither of them could wait to leave all the blood and deaths behind. It was going to be beautiful.

Chapter Twenty-Seven

Two Months Later…

It was a lovely day on Miami Beach. Ocean water washed against the sands, then receded back again. Emperor and Ayana walked barefoot down the shore, holding hands, looking out at the sunshine.

Although still somewhat emotionally broken, they decided it was best to try to put the past behind them. At least for now, anyway.

After burying Juan, the two of them, along with Carmena and Smoke, all moved to Miami to begin a new life together.

A few weeks later, Ayana discovered that she was pregnant with her first child, and Emperor thought it was best for them to leave Detroit for a while, at least until their baby was born. They could always go back and get Claudia.

Emperor's parents loved Ayana and couldn't wait to finally meet their grandchild. If it was a boy, they planned to name the baby Juan, after his uncle.

Carmena and Smoke were taking their time to really get to know each other. Smoke was actually considering settling down with her and having some children of his own, now that Emperor was about to have one.

Things seemed to be looking up for all of them. They figured they would wait it out for a year or so, then go back to Detroit to finish what was undone. Claudia wasn't going to get away with what she had done. Juan's death wouldn't go unpunished. No matter how long it took, or what type of resources they needed, Claudia was going to pay… And the only means of compensation would be made by her blood.

*****

Special Agent Nero Jackson walked into the Miami-Dade Police Department. In his hand, he carried a manila file. He took an elevator to the fifth floor, got off, then walked up to the main desk, where there was a uniformed officer seated, signing documents.

The uniformed cop looked him up and down, taking in the black suit, pressed white shirt, and black tie. "How may I help you?" he asked skeptically.

"How you doin'… I'm Special Agent Nero Jackson with the Federal Bureau of Investigation. I just flew in from Detroit. I need to see one of your homicide detectives…" he said, looking at one of the papers in the file. "Detective Arielo Rodriguez. Is he in?"

"Just a second. Let me check, please." The frail, blond-haired officer picked up the phone and dialed a number. He said a couple things, nodded a few times, then hung up. "All right, Agent Jackson, he'll be right out."

He smiled a stiff, but friendly, smile. "Thank you."

A few seconds went past, then Detective Arielo Rodriguez appeared from around the corner.

"Agent Jackson," he said, shaking his hand. "What can I do for you?"

"Can we go in your office, please?"

"Certainly."

They walked up the hall, then took a hard left turn and landed in Rodriguez's office.

Agent Jackson walked in and closed the door behind him. "Detective Rodriguez, do you recall working a case years ago involving two young Colombian guys mixed up in a bloody war with several local Colombian drug cartels here in Miami?"

Detective Rodriguez took a seat in his chair, then offered Agent Jackson a seat in the chair across from him.

"No. I'm all right, thank you."

"Sure. Yeah, I remember the case… I was captured by it. Two kids taking on the cartels… robbing and killing them. Sure, I remember…" He leaned back in the chair, his chin high, staring at the ceiling. "What were their names again?"

Agent Jackson walked up and slammed the file on the desk. "Here, let me refresh your memory…" Agent Jackson opened the folder so the detective could see the photos inside. "Emperor Juarez and Tsun Guzman, also known as Smoke."

Rodriguez sat up, arms over the desk. "That's right. I remember them both well. I never seen two young men so loyal to each other. I was impressed. I mean, we tried everything to get them to flip on one another, but they wouldn't. You couldn't even get them to speak. I never seen anything like it in all my years of being a detective. In the end, they walked right out of here and we couldn't touch them. They made a lot of fans over at the Miami Herald. The reporters got a kick out of their story. Some people looked at them like heroes. Some seen them as …"

"Murderers," Agent Jackson said flatly, cutting him off. "Murderers. Both of them. And unlike your department, I won't rest until both of them are in jail for the rest of their lives, or looking at an execution date on death row."

Rodriguez straightened up. "So, what is it you need from me?"

Agent Jackson smiled. "I want to know everything it is that you know about these two, so I can begin to understand how they think. That way, when it's time, I'll be able to catch them. And let me assure you, Detective Rodriguez, once I catch them, there won't be no escaping charges. There won't be any walking out. There will only be death or life in prison. Is that understood?"

"Clearly."

To Be Continued....

ABOUT THE AUTHOR

I grew up in Detroit, Michigan, and started hustling when I was 12 years old, selling heroin and crack cocaine for older drug dealers around my neighborhood. I dropped out of school in the 9th grade and began hustling for myself when I was 15.

By the time I was 16 years old I was making thousands of dollars a day. Soon my craving for fast money increased and I began to recruit soldiers and travel to other cities to sell cocaine and crack cocaine.

I made my first million dollars in Indianapolis, Indiana then went to Charleston, West Virginia and became the king of crack cocaine.

It was my vision for my crew and I to be separate from other drug organizations so we began to call ourselves "Junior Cartel," … I created a set of rules and principles for all of us to live by, and we grew into a family, making more money than any of us ever dreamed or believed was possible."

I spent the next 14 and a half years of my life behind bars paying for my crimes. While I was incarcerated I began to educated myself in science, social studies, history, finance, mathematics, and writing. I was released in March of 2015.

I've been working on getting my life together but struggle every day like many people who live in the neighborhood I'm from. I now live in Detroit, Michigan where I fight to change my life. This is my first book, but it won't be my last.

Andolian Napraja

Made in the USA
Lexington, KY
15 May 2018